Sempringham Studies

Germany 1916-1941

E.J. Feuchtwanger

Sempringham *publishing,* Bedford

Cover picture. A poster from November 1932. Papen is ironically applauded for the emergency decrees, cutting wages, pensions and wage bargaining, so giving support to the Communist Party, but Hitler can save Germany from Bolshevism. (Courtesy of Weidenfeld and Nicolson Archives.)

Sempringham Studies are distributed to booksellers by
Central Books, 99 Wallis Road, London E9 5LN Tel. 0181-986 4854.

Sempringham Books are available to schools, colleges and individuals direct: Sempringham Books, PO Box 248, Bedford MK41 0ZU.

ISBN 0 9515764 6 1

First published 1997

Impression number 10 9 8 7 6 5 4 3 2 1
Year 2001 2000 1999 1998 1997

Designed and set by Sempringham publishing services, Bedford.
Line portraits by Stephen Odom.
Sempringham publishing, PO Box 248, Bedford MK41 0ZU.
Printed by Redwood Books, Trowbridge, Wiltshire.

Contents

To student readers and their tutors

Ways to use this book

This book looks at Germany, the state at the centre of European History this century, a History which included the creation of a ruthless dictatorship by Hitler. The core chapters, 5 - 9, outline the events of German History, offer reasons for them, disect how Hitler built his power and invite you to develop your own analysis. As you read, list the strengths and weaknesses of the Weimar Republic (Chapter 5), the reasons for the achievement of power, in 1933, by the Nazis (Chapters 5 and 6) and the main features of Nazi rule (Chapters 7 and 8) and phases of foreign policy (Chapter 9) and identify steps of development for each issue. For comments on how to use information to develop your analysis and prepare essay answers you will find guidelines in Chapters 4, 6 and 7 of *The Good History Students' Handbook,* Sempringham, 1993, and Chapters 3, 6 and 7 of *Undergraduate History Study - The Guide,* Sempringham, 1997.

To understand the History of Germany after 1918 you need to have an appreciation of issues and events before that time. These are outlined in Chapters 1, 2 and 4. Even if you use the core chapters first, you are advised to read these chapters, especially Chapter 4, before you finish your German topic. You may decide to make less detailed notes on these earlier chapters.

It is easy to read about the past and to forget that it was people, living, scheming, commanding, fighting, who lived through, and made, the events recounted in History books. Chapter 3 focuses on eleven main personalities, summarises their part in the events, and seeks to bring them to life.

Chapter 10 summarises the ongoing debate among historians about these years. Information from this chapter is helpful when answers require a historiographical approach.

In order to gain an initial overview of these years it is a good idea to read quickly Chapter 11, for a first time, before you read the core chapters, 5 - 9.

1 Overview and Issues

From Imperial Germany to the Third Reich

The first half of the twentieth century was dominated by the two world wars, 1914 to 1918 and 1939 to 1945. These two wars, the first modern total wars, were devastating in their consequences and almost everything else flowed from them and their side effects. Nowhere was this more so than in Germany. Imperial Germany, also sometimes called the Second Reich, the first being the medieval German Reich overthrown by Napoleon in 1806, came to an end with military defeat and revolution in November 1918. The flight of the Kaiser, Wilhelm II, spelt the end of the imperial, as well as of the twenty or so lesser monarchies in Germany (see page 30). A republican, parliamentary, democratic regime, known as the Weimar Republic, was established. It was always heavily overshadowed by the fact that it arose from defeat and national humiliation. Its ultimate failure was, however, never inevitable. Two economic catastrophes, the Great Inflation culminating in 1923 (see page 54), and the Great Depression, reaching its lowest point in 1932 (see page 72), deeply affected the lives of all Germans. In the minds of many of them these disasters were closely linked to the German defeat of 1918 and to the Treaty of Versailles imposed by the victorious Allies. The Weimar Republic was able to overcome the first of these great social and economic crises. From 1924 to 1929 it enjoyed a more stable and prosperous period. The second crisis, however, proved too much for it. It made the National Socialist Party, led by Adolf Hitler, into a mass movement, and by 1932 into the largest German party, though without an absolute majority.

Hitler's appointment as Chancellor on 30 January 1933 (see page 82) marks the end of the Weimar Republic and the beginning of the Third Reich. It was one of the two great totalitarian dictatorships of the twentieth century, the other being the Bolshevik regime established by Lenin in 1917. Both Nazism and Communism were attempts to create radically new societies, based on a reshaping of human nature itself. Both were catastrophic failures and caused untold human suffering. In the case of Nazi Germany, the central idea was that the superior German, or Aryan race, would through conquest create an empire, ultimately world-wide, that would last a thousand years. Inferior races, such as the Slavs of Eastern Europe, would be reduced to slave status in this empire. The Jews, regarded as a sort of counter-race, feeding like parasites on the Aryan master race, would be eliminated. The same fate would also be meted out to groups like gypsies or the mentally and physically handicapped, who threatened the health of the master race. This was the vision that motivated Hitler and the history of the Third Reich is the story how he and his fellow-Nazis came close to realising it in all its terrible consequences. War was always an integral part of the Nazi ideology and within six years of attaining power Hitler had unleashed it. As a result the Third Reich hurtled to self-destruction. With it some 55 million perished world-wide and the German nation state, started in 1871, came to an end in 1945.

Issues

These dramatic events in Germany have produced an enormous amount of writing by historians and they still shape many attitudes in the present. As a result 1933 has often been seen as the central date in German history. The arrival in power and acceptance of so barbaric a regime and an ideology as Hitler's in an apparently civilised country needs a great deal of explaining. Even events like the Great Depression, referred to earlier, can only partially explain it, for other countries, for example the United States, were equally affected by this world-wide breakdown of the economic system without losing their democratic institutions. Historians have therefore argued that there was a special German path (*Sonderweg* in German), which caused democratic and liberal attitudes to be less well developed than they were in the major Western democracies, particularly Britain. Others have cast doubt on this interpretation, arguing that each nation had particular features in its development. Parliamentary democracy was certainly not fully developed in Imperial Germany (see page 9) but, by and large, the rule of law prevailed. When a democratic system was fully established after 1918 it was not in favourable circumstances.

Even if the rise of the Third Reich is mainly accounted for by the internal history and circumstances of Germany, the external situation of the country must also form an important element in the interpretation of her history as a unified state. Germany is a geographical expression and has no clear boundaries. If speaking German as a mother tongue is to be taken as a criterion, then all of what after 1918 became Austria, and considerable parts of what became Poland and Czechoslovakia, would have to be included in the Reich. This is exactly what Hitler claimed in the early phases of his territorial expansion and others had claimed it before him. Even without these additions Germany was the most populous state in Europe after 1871, west of the much less developed Russia. She could, therefore, aspire to predominance in Europe but, as the two world wars showed, she was not ultimately strong enough to impose this pre-dominance against the opposition of the other great powers of Europe as well as of the USA.

Chronological Table

1871-1914

1871	18 Jan	Proclamation of German Empire at Versailles
1890	15 March	Fall of Bismarck
1909	July	Bethmann Hollweg becomes Chancellor
1911		Second Morocco Crisis: Germany fails to secure territorial gains
1912	12 Jan	Reichstag elections make SPD largest party

1914

28 June	Assassination of Archduke Franz Ferdinand at Sarajevo
1 Aug	German declaration of war on Russia
4 Aug	SPD votes for war credits in Reichstag
Sept	Falkenhayn succeeds Moltke as Commander in Chief

1916

29 Aug	Hindenburg and Ludendorff take over OHL (Supreme Command)

1917

Feb	Unrestricted submarine warfare
6 April	USA declares war on Germany
12 July	Fall of Bethmann Hollweg
19 July	Peace resolution passed by Reichstag.

1918

Jan	Strikes in Berlin
3 March	Treaty of Brest-Litovsk with Russia. Peace on Eastern Front
21 March	Ludendorff's offensive starts in the West
8 Aug	'Black day' of the German Army. British armies regain territory lost in the spring
28 Sept	Ludendorff demands armistice
3 Oct	Prince Max of Baden becomes Chancellor. Request for armistice sent to President Wilson
28 Oct	Constitutional changes promulgated
3 Nov	Mutiny in the German Navy
7 Nov	Fall of Bavarian monarchy
9 Nov	Ebert takes over from Prince Max. Kaiser abdicates.
16 Dec	Congress of Workers and Soldiers Councils meets in Berlin and decides on immediate elections for a Constituent Assembly

1919

Jan	Spartacist rising in Berlin
15 Jan	Murder of Karl Liebknecht and Rosa Luxemburg
19 Jan	Elections for a Constituent Assembly
28 June	Treaty of Versailles signed
11 Aug	Weimar Constitution comes into force

1920

24 Feb	Foundation meeting of NSDAP in Munich

13-17 March	Kapp Putsch fails
6 June	First Reichstag elections of Republic

1922

16 April	Treaty of Rapallo signed with Russia

1923

11 Jan	French occupation of Ruhr begins
13 Aug	Stresemann becomes Chancellor
Sept	End of passive resistance in Ruhr
9 Nov	Hitler's Beer Hall Putsch in Munich fails
15 Nov	Rentenmark introduced. Inflation ended

1924

April	Hitler receives five-year sentence. Writes *Mein Kampf* in prison
4 May	Second Reichstag elections
Aug	Dawes Plan accepted. Helps economic recovery
7 Dec	Third Reichstag elections

1925

Feb	NSDAP refounded
28 Feb	Death of Ebert
April	Hindenburg elected President
Oct	Locarno treaties create greater security in Europe

1926

Sept	Germany joins League of Nations

1927

	Unemployment Insurance Law enacted

1928

20 May	Fourth Reichstag elections
June	Great Coalition headed by SPD

1929

June	Young Plan proposals for reparations
3 Oct	Death of Stresemann
24 Oct	Wall Street Crash starts world-wide slump

1930

27 March	Great Coalition falls
30 March	Brüning becomes Chancellor
14 Sept	Fifth Reichstag elections. NSDAP becomes second-largest party

1931

13 July	Major German bank suspends payments
11 Oct	Harzburg meeting of Nazis and national opposition

1932

13 March	First presidential ballot

10 April	Hindenburg re-elected President
13 April	Ban on SA by Reich Government
30 May	Brüning forced to resign as Chancellor
1 June	Franz von Papen becomes Chancellor
20 July	Prussian Government driven from office
31 July	Sixth Reichstag elections. NSDAP becomes largest party
6 Nov	Seventh Reichstag elections. Heavy Nazi losses
2 Dec	Schleicher becomes Chancellor

1933

4 Jan	Meeting of Papen and Hitler in Cologne
28 Jan	Schleicher resigns
30 Jan	Hitler becomes Chancellor
27 Feb	Reichstag fire
28 Feb	Presidential decree suspends civil liberties
5 March	Last Reichstag elections
13 March	Goebbels becomes Reich Minister for Propaganda and Popular Enlightenment
21 March	Day of Potsdam
23 March	Enabling Act passed. Reichstag surrenders legislative power to Hitler Cabinet
1 April	National boycott of Jewish shops
7 April	Law permits dismissal of civil servants on political and racial grounds
2 May	Free Trade Unions dissolved
10 May	Burning of Books
14 July	NSDAP becomes only legal party
12 Nov	Plebiscite approves Germany's withdrawal from League of Nations

1934

26 Jan	German-Polish Non-Aggression Pact
17 June	Papen's Marburg speech. Hitler visits Mussolini in Venice
30 June	Night of the Long Knives. Röhm and SA leaders shot
25 July	Nazi rising in Vienna. Mussolini moves troops to the Brenner
2 Aug	Hitler succeeds Hindenburg as Head of State, with title Führer and Reich Chancellor

1935

13 Jan	Saar votes in League of Nations plebiscite to return to Germany
16 March	Conscription reintroduced in Germany
18 June	Anglo-German Naval Agreement
15 Sept	Nuremberg Laws announced

1936

7 March	German troops enter Rhineland demilitarised zone
11 July	German-Austrian treaty leaves Austria in German sphere of influence
25 July	Hitler decides to support Franco in Spanish Civil War
Aug	Hitler's Four-Year Plan Memorandum on economic preparations for war
1 Nov	Berlin-Rome Axis announced by Mussolini

1937

Sept	Mussolini's state visit to Germany
5 Nov	Hossbach Memorandum records meeting of Hitler and armed services leaders. Hitler reveals plans for territorial expansion
26 Nov	Schacht resigns as Minister of Economics

1938

4 Feb	Resignation of Blomberg, Fritsch and Neurath announced
13 March	German troops enter Austria
30 May	Hitler issues directive 'Case Green', military action against Czechoslovakia
15 Sept	Chamberlain's first meeting with Hitler
29 Sept	Munich Agreement returns Sudetenland to Germany
9/10 Nov	Anti-Jewish Pogrom (Kristallnacht)

1939

15 March	Remainder of Czechoslovakia occupied by German troops
31 March	British guarantee to Poland and Rumania
23 Aug	Nazi-Soviet Pact
1 Sept	German troops invade Poland
3 Sept	Britain and France declare war on Germany

1940

9 April	German troops invade Denmark and Norway
10 May	German offensive in the West begins
22 June	French-German armistice signed
15 Sept	Climax of Battle of Britain

1941

6 April	German attack on Yugoslavia and Greece
22 June	Operation Barbarossa - German attack on Russia
5 Dec	Soviet counter-offensive around Moscow
7 Dec	Japan attacks USA at Pearl Harbor
11 Dec	Germany declares war on USA

1942

20 Jan	Wannsee conference on 'final solution' of 'Jewish question'
4 Nov	British break-through at El Alamein
19 Nov	Soviet counter-offensive at Stalingrad begins

1943

30 Jan	German Sixth Army capitulates at Stalingrad
25 July	Fall of Mussolini

1944

6 June	D-Day landing in Normandy
20 July	Failure of assassination attempt on Hitler

1945

30 April	Hitler commits suicide in Berlin bunker
8 May	Germany surrenders

2 Background: Imperial Germany

Causes of the Two World Wars

The two world wars were the crucial upheavals of the twentieth century and Germany was at the centre of both of them. If one had to pick out the single most obvious cause of the two wars, it would be the fact that it proved difficult for the society of European nation states to adjust to the arrival of a powerful newcomer, Germany. To put it this way is to give priority to the external relations of the German nation state that came into existence in 1871. In recent years historians have increasingly emphasised the importance of Germany's internal development in explaining the causes of the two world wars. They have seen the internal and external developments as inextricably intermixed and have pointed out that domestic tensions often became the motive for decisions in foreign policy. This is called the primacy of domestic politics. The older, nationalist school of German historians talked of the primacy of foreign policy, arguing that their country, in the centre of Europe, had always to assert itself against the potential enemies surrounding it and that this was the key to the course of events. The external threat was used as an argument for authoritarian government and against democracy and parliamentary government. This approach, with its implication that Germany's conduct was defensive, became much less tenable after the Second World War, in which Germany, controlled by Hitler, was clearly the aggressor. The roots of National Socialism had to be sought mainly in Germany and not outside. Here we are concerned chiefly with Germany's domestic development, but how this interacted with Germany's external situation will also be a major theme.

Total War in 1916

The First World War had already lasted two years. It had become clear that it was not the kind of limited war common in the nineteenth century, but a total war, involving all the human and material resources of the combatant countries. Such a war was very difficult to control or to end without the complete victory of one side or the other. The sacrifices demanded of the nations at war, the sufferings of their peoples and the emotions aroused were so great that a negotiated or compromise peace, such as had ended many previous wars, was almost impossible. The masses were now participating fully in politics, a development speeded by the arrival of mass media, in the first instance popular newspapers. The rulers and governments of the warring countries therefore found themselves embarked upon a course which was taking them into unknown territory, a course which was to prove fatal for those on the losing side and which was damaging even to the victors. Historians have ever since had to ask the question how so universally disastrous a situation could have arisen.

The European State System since 1871

The arrival of Germany among the Great Powers of Europe was the biggest change in the affairs of Europe since the Napoleonic wars. Bismarck was more than any other single person responsible. He remained in power as German Chancellor for another twenty years after 1870. Having largely engineered the wars that brought Germany into being, he was from 1871 until his fall in 1890 mainly concerned to ensure the safety and stability both at home and abroad of his creation. In the European concert of powers Germany under his rule became, on the whole, a factor for peace, though he was not above using the threat of war when it suited him.

Bismarck was much less successful in ensuring stability at home. The creation of a unified economic area in the centre of Europe unleashed a dynamic rise of population and production, as the following table shows:

Table 2: Population and comparative coal and steel production

Population (in millions)		
1871	1891	1911
40,997	49,762	65,359

	Production (in millions of tons)	
	1890	1913
	Coal	*Coal*
Germany	70,200	191,500
Britain	184,000	292,000
	Steel	*Steel*
Germany	2,195	18,654
Britain	3,579	6,903

Germany's industrialisation, much more rapid than Britain's at an earlier stage, produced great changes and pressures in German society, which the political system shaped by Bismarck, mainly to ensure his own survival, was increasingly unable to contain. These pressures, particularly the rise of a numerous urban industrial working class and a party mainly based on this class, the Social Democratic Party of Germany (SPD), contributed to Bismarck's fall. His successors between 1890 and 1914 were lesser men and faced the same problems in aggravated form. To understand their problems, we need to take a look at the constitutional and political system of Imperial Germany, which remained unchanged in essentials until it was overthrown by Germany's defeat in 1918.

The Political System of Imperial Germany 1871-1918

The most important feature of the German system, distinguishing it from Britain's fully parliamentary system, was that the Reich Chancellor, equivalent to the British Prime Minister, held office not on the basis of a parliamentary majority, but was appointed by the Emperor. The German parliament, the Reichstag, was essential for the passing of laws and the granting of money, not unlike the British House of Commons, but it could not make or unmake governments. On the other hand the Reichstag was elected by universal manhood suffrage, all men over 25 having the vote, a franchise considerably wider than that in force in Britain up to 1918. As a result mass parties, with large organisations for the purpose of fighting elections, had grown up, as in Britain. German politics at the national level revolved chiefly around the problem how successive chancellors, appointed by the Emperor and not representative of parliamentary parties, could obtain the majorities for the legislative and financial measures they considered necessary for the country. This task was greatly complicated by the fact that in the last Reichstag elections before the war, in 1912, the SPD had become much the largest party, with more than a third of the vote.

The Social Democrats

The powerful German SPD was totally excluded from any share in the national government. The Emperor had publicly called the Social Democrats unpatriotic, its members were severely discriminated against in the recruitment of all branches of the public service, including even the railways. August Bebel, the leader of the SPD for nearly fifty years until his death in 1913, was known as 'the Emperor of German Socialism', the counterpart of the actual Emperor, Wilhelm II. When Bebel toured the country people held up their small children in the crowd so that they could see him. Yet, shortly before his death, he recorded his astonishment when, in the corridors of the Reichstag, the Chancellor, for the first time ever, recognised him and inquired after his health. On paper the SPD was a party dedicated to the overthrow of the capitalist system by revolution, along the lines envisaged by Karl Marx. In practice the SPD had become a reformist party, not unlike the Labour Party in this country, adapted to winning power through elections. The reformist or revisionist, as opposed to the revolutionary tendency in the SPD was strengthened by the fact that most German workers felt they had a great deal more to lose than their chains. Bismarck, in an unsuccessful bid to take 'the wind out of the sails of the socialists', had already laid the foundations of the modern welfare state by introducing accident insurance and old age pensions and his successors had developed the system further. The German working man, in spite of the discrimination practised against him, was therefore loyal and patriotic.

The Middle Classes and their Parties

The rise of the Social Democrats greatly alarmed not only the governing classes in Germany, but also broad sections of the middle class. Up to the end of the nineteenth century the German political parties had been slow to adjust to the arrival of a mass electorate. The only exception was the Centre Party, which had in many ways foreshadowed the rise of the SPD. It arose in response to Bismarck's persecution of Roman Catholicism in the 1870s and was entirely based on the Catholic part of the population, about 35% of the total, concentrated in areas like the Rhineland and Bavaria. The other parties were in their organisations and methods still stuck in the era preceding the introduction of universal suffrage. The Liberals had been split by Bismarck's success in unifying Germany. The weakness of liberalism was to remain an on-going and significant feature of the German scene.

The Conservatives were also divided into several parties and also found it difficult to adjust to the beginnings of a democratic system, in which they did not in any case believe. They had, however, some advantages. One was that conservatism was the prevailing view among all those who made up the governing classes in the narrower sense, namely the Emperor and his court and advisers, the military, the aristocratic landowners in the eastern provinces of Prussia, known as the Junkers, and the leaders of heavy industry, particularly coal and steel. In addition Prussia, which comprised about two-thirds of the population and territory of Germany, gave them a strong political base. Prussia, like the other states making up Germany, such as Bavaria and Saxony, had its own parliament, which still controlled many important areas, such as education and the police. For the election of the Prussian parliament, the Landtag, a much more restrictive franchise prevailed than for the Reichstag, the so-called three-tier franchise, which was not secret. Those who paid the most taxes had the most voting power. The Conservatives therefore had an entrenched position in the Prussian Landtag, where the SPD remained very weak. Another feature of Imperial Germany that has always been stressed by historians was the strong position of the military and the hold that military values had right through the middle classes. The Reichstag had limited control over military affairs and the chiefs of the Army, later also of the Navy, were responsible directly to the Emperor. At the higher levels of the bourgeoisie a commission in the reserve army was considered the most desirable social distinction. The chancellor often appeared in uniform, something unthinkable for a British prime minister.

The Patriotic Leagues

All this could not alter the fact that those groups in society other than

Catholics supporting the Centre Party and workers supporting the SPD had increasingly to be mobilised for political action. Much of this was done around the turn of the century, not by the conservative or liberal parties in the Reichstag directly, but by so-called leagues, organisations that used strongly nationalist propaganda to appeal to public opinion. One of the first to use such methods was the Agrarian League, founded as early as 1892, to mobilise farmers throughout Germany against liberal trading policies and to defend them against being overwhelmed in an urban industrial society. It aroused emotions against many aspects of modern city life, which it portrayed as decadent, in contrast to the healthy life of the countryside rooted in traditional ways. Jews were singled out as particularly guilty in promoting the negative, parasitic side of international capitalism. Some of the literature put out by the Agrarian League reads like an early version of the propaganda later produced by the Nazis. The Pan-German League, although not very large in numbers, advocated the idea of Germans, whether inside or outside the Reich, as a race destined for world power. The Navy League had the largest membership and was originally promoted by Tirpitz, the admiral who had persuaded the Kaiser to build an ocean-going navy to rival the British. Although the Imperial Government welcomed these leagues as a counterweight to the labour movement, it did not control them.

What had therefore come into existence in the decade before 1914 was a large body of organised public opinion that wished Germany to assume a leading place not only in Europe but on a world scale. They wanted to see their country claim 'its place in the sun', a stark contrast to the socialist slogan 'workers of the world, unite!'. Much of the mass support for nationalism, imperialism and militarism represented by the leagues came from the social groups who felt themselves to be losers in the changes which were transforming their country at breakneck speed into a modern industrial nation, small farmers, shopkeepers, artisans and master craftsmen. Theirs was a nationalism tinged with resentment. Historians have tended to emphasise the negative side of both Bismarckian and Wilhelmine society, because it ended up in the disasters of war, defeat and revolution. More recently the balance has been somewhat redressed by drawing attention to many positive features, such as an educational system that was the envy of other countries, a very lively forward-looking artistic scene and a strong element of social criticism which attacked the spirit of militarism and chauvinism.

Impact of the German Domestic Situation on Foreign Policy

The German Government saw a successful foreign and imperial policy, such as was demanded by the nationalist section of opinion, as an antidote to the threat of socialism at home. The pursuit of predominance in Europe and of world power, as exemplified by the naval building programme, was not only an end in itself, but was a deliberate policy of social imperialism, an attempt to bridge class differences at home by prestigious gains abroad. Inevitably such a policy, contrasting with the cautious course pursued by Bismarck, alarmed the other Great Powers of the day. Increasingly the Germans felt themselves encircled, a situation largely brought about by their own actions and inept diplomacy. In the years before 1914 their only remaining major ally was Austria-Hungary, an empire itself acutely threatened with disintegration by the forces of nationalism. Far from achieving the place 'in the sun', which they thought was their due, the Germans found themselves in a deteriorating position.

This created a frame of mind among Germany's civilian and military policy-makers which regarded war increasingly as inevitable and toyed with the idea of a preventive war, the notion that a war should be fought sooner rather than later, before there was a further deterioration of Germany's diplomatic and military circumstances. Domestically, the nationalist section of opinion put the Government under great pressure to secure spectacular successes in foreign policy. In domestic politics the contending forces became locked in stalemate. The parties in the Reichstag were unable and unwilling to achieve a breakthrough into fully-fledged parliamentarianism, nor was any progress made towards modifying the Prussian three-tier franchise, insistently demanded by the SPD. On the other hand the wilder plans of the extreme nationalists, to carry out a coup to curtail or abolish the popularly elected Reichstag, could not be put into practice without risking a civil war. Bethmann Hollweg, the Chancellor since 1909, tried to carry out what he called a policy of the diagonal, namely a balance between the extremes. It satisfied neither side, but the Emperor, whose own prestige was gravely damaged, maintained him in office. In foreign policy Bethmann Hollweg was conciliatory towards Britain, but it proved impossible to end the competitive naval rearmament.

3 Key Personalities, 1916-1941

Kaiser Wilhelm II

In interpreting history long-term tendencies and underlying dispositions are very important, but the impact of personalities should never be underestimated. To use an analogy, the historical landscape is a given fact, but what is made of it depends on personalities. At the start of our story the Kaiser, Wilhelm II, who was born in 1859, a grandson of Queen Victoria, and came to the throne in 1888, was still a significant, though increasingly discredited, figure. In his arrogance, boastfulness and instability he personified some of the less attractive traits of the country over which he ruled. He was not unintelligent and had a quick grasp and good memory. This impressed many who came into contact with him, especially as he was so highly placed a personage, but he lacked application and was influenced by the last person he saw. He moved around restlessly and became known as the *Reisekaiser,* the travelling Emperor. He was given to playing tasteless and infantile practical jokes on members of his entourage. Above all, his many ill-considered initiatives and pronouncements did a great deal of damage over the years. By 1914 he had perpetrated so many gaffes that he had lost self-confidence. The task of co-ordinating the whole governmental machine, which the constitution placed upon him, had always been beyond him. The war relegated him to a backseat, without making his theoretically central role totally redundant, a particularly unfortunate combination.

Field Marshal Paul von Hindenburg

During the war the Kaiser's place as the symbol of Germany was increasingly taken by Field Marshal Paul von Hindenburg. Born in 1847 he had a moderately distinguished career in the Prussian Army, retiring as a general in 1911. He had seen active service only as a very junior officer in 1866 and 1870. Recalled in 1914, the victory of Tannenberg (see page 21) made him into a national hero. His chief British biographer called him the Wooden Titan and his ability was certainly limited. His impressive physical appearance, of which he made the most, generated a feeling of confidence and unshakeable resolve. This was the image to which many Germans clung in the many disasters afflicting their country during the remainder of Hindenburg's life, regardless of the fact that he played a part in bringing these disasters about. Thus he became in 1925, at the age of 77, a somewhat reluctant candidate for the Presidency of the Republic. At some crucial junctures he displayed less than complete loyalty to men who had put their trust in him. The worst service he rendered Germany was to appoint Hitler Chancellor in January 1933. By then a very old man of 85, he was reluctantly persuaded to do so by those around him.

Erich Ludendorff

Erich Ludendorff was the real brains behind Hindenburg in the First World War, but was abandoned by his chief in the hour of defeat. He was born in 1865 and coming from a middle-class background he was an unusual figure in the still mainly aristocratic corps of senior army officers but his role in capturing the Belgian fortress of Liège in August 1914 brought him prominence. He became Hindenburg's Chief of Staff in the task of halting the Russian invasion of East Prussia. He remained with Hindenburg, with the title Quarter-Master General, when the latter took overall command on 29 August 1916. From this point until his dismissal on 26 October 1918 Ludendorff was the virtual dictator of Germany. He displayed some of the same characteristics as his successor Hitler twenty years later. He believed that sheer willpower and brute force could solve all problems. Lantern-jawed, his appearance expressed his utter determination, but it only served to drive his country into total military defeat. He had to flee Germany for a while after the collapse of 1918, but returned to play a role in extreme nationalist right-wing politics. Thus, he became involved with the Nazi movement and was included in the government which Hitler attempted to proclaim in the Munich Beer Hall Putsch of November 1923 (see page 55). Ludendorff was the most prestigious figure on the radical right, but Hitler managed to sideline him after 1925.

The Weimar Period

Friedrich Ebert

The Weimar Republic was short of colourful political personalities that could have made parliamentary democracy more attractive to the people. At least three men stand out because of the importance of the decisions they had to take. Friedrich Ebert was the first President of the Weimar Republic and the central figure in the events following Germany's defeat in 1918. He came from the German working class, a saddler by trade, and rose to prominence as the leader of the SPD. Because he was ordinary in appearance and did not dress up in gaudy uniforms, as the captains and kings of pre-war Germany had done, he was ridiculed by the opponents of the republic. Pictures of him taken in bathing trunks in 1919 were used to disparage the new regime. Worse than that, he had frequently, even when President, to defend himself against scurrilous accusations that as a socialist leader he had undermined Germany's will to fight in the First World War. This contributed to his early death in 1925. Nothing could have been further from the truth, because he was a man of great patriotism who, more than anybody, helped to preserve the integrity of Germany as a country after 1918. If there was a weakness, it was that he was too trusting of the old military and civil elites, whose assistance he sought in governing the country amid the difficult circumstances of defeat and revolution. On the whole, he acquitted himself with distinction and, above all, with decency, if not always with greatness, in taking key decisions, for which there were no precedents to guide him.

Gustav Stresemann

In the middle years of Weimar Gustav Stresemann, born in 1878, emerged as the most conspicuous leader. Bullet-headed, cigar-smoking, but also a compelling spokesman for peace and reconciliation, he seemed to personify Germany to the world in the 1920s. He came from humble beginnings and had risen before 1914 as the administrator of a federation of German industries, mostly those engaged in newer, more export-orientated branches. Thus, he became a leader of the more right-wing of the two Liberal parties of the imperial period. He was a strong nationalist and believed in Germany's destiny as a great political and economic world power. He was so tainted with support for expansionist policies that the more left-wing and internationally minded liberals would not have him in their party after 1918. It was one of the reasons why it proved impossible to unite all liberals in one party in the Weimar Republic. Stresemann was a monarchist at heart, but he became the prime example of those who have been called republicans by reason (*Vernunftrepublikaner*). Reason told him that a restoration of the monarchy was unlikely in the 1920s and that the recovery of Germany as a power could not come by military means. It was this realism that made him so powerful a politician. The struggle to make such reasonableness prevail against the emotionally charged nationalist resentment of the Weimar period undermined his health and he died prematurely in October 1929. We will never know whether he could have saved Germany from Hitler.

• Gustav Stresemann

Heinrich Brüning

In the final phase of the republic Heinrich Brüning was Chancellor for two crucial years and tragically failed to save Germany from the rising tide of National Socialism. Born in 1885, he had risen through the Catholic Centre Party and its trade union wing. He belonged to the younger generation of politically active Catholics, who were concerned to get rid of the feeling, still prevalent in Imperial Germany, that Catholics were second-class citizens. Brüning had, like so many others, been deeply shaped by the experience of fighting as a young officer in the trenches of the First World War. He came to the fore in the Reichstag of the 1920s as the financial expert of his party. It was this and his strong nationalism that recommended him to Hindenburg and his advisers as a potential chancellor in 1929. Great efforts were made during his chancellorship to give Brüning the image of a strong leader, to counter the attraction of that other leader or Führer, Hitler. Brüning as a person and politician was, however, the very opposite of a demagogue like Hitler. A soft-spoken bachelor, wearing gold-rimmed glasses, who shunned anything flamboyant, he thought that constant belt-tightening measures, however painful, would be accepted simply because they were, in his view, necessary.

General Kurt von Schleicher

General Kurt von Schleicher was the adviser of Hindenburg most responsible for picking Brüning. He also picked the next chancellor, Papen, and then himself became the last chancellor before Hitler. He was therefore a key figure in the events that led to the Third Reich. He was an officer in the General Staff, who acquired a reputation as a political expert and fixer. That the German Army, the Reichswehr, as it was called in the Weimar period, and limited, as it was by the Treaty of Versailles, to a strength of 100,000 officers and men, needed someone like Schleicher to play its political cards, shows how strange the position of the military was in Germany. They considered themselves the permanent embodiment of the nation, while the republic, for which they had little time, was only its temporary form. Schleicher became so powerful, because he was on friendly terms with Hindenburg and his son. When the old President lost confidence in Schleicher, whom he had always called 'my dear young friend', his influence ended and within days Hitler was chancellor. Schleicher's fellow officers had also got fed up with the way in which his position had dragged the Army openly into politics. They hoped that the formation of the Hitler Cabinet would allow them to withdraw backstage, while continuing to determine the policies that concerned them. Schleicher was a man who liked to work behind the scenes and he assumed the chancellorship only when all else had failed. He was a man alternating between moods of elation and depression. He boasted that he pulled all the strings in the whole political show. In fact he was engaged in a deadly game and his failure led, quite apart from anything else, to his own murder in 1934, along with his wife.

The Third Reich

Adolf Hitler

So we arrive at the Third Reich. Hitler was its central figure and the most recent historiography has not changed that view, although the limits of his power are also rightly emphasised. The ordinary German did not so much believe in the details of the Nazi ideology, as in the myth of Hitler as the miracle worker who, so it appeared, had revived the German economy, reversed the humiliations of Versailles and brought large tracts of German-inhabited territory back into the Reich without firing a shot. Even when it came to war, which many Germans feared, Hitler won easy victories, culminating in the sensational triumph over France in 1940. The Hitler myth was created by the propaganda machine of Goebbels, but up to 1941 the successes were so great that propaganda had an easy task. The hardships imposed, let alone the crimes committed by the regime were pushed out of mind. When after 1941 it became increasingly obvious that Hitler was driving his country towards a catastrophe in which every German man, woman and child would suffer severely, many still found it hard 'to say goodbye to the Führer'.

Undoubtedly, Hitler had a combination of qualities that enabled him, in times that were out of joint, to make a huge, though in the end almost entirely destructive impact. He had a very sharp tactical sense in politics. At the same time he clung to his guiding ideas with great fanaticism. His gifts as an agitator enabled him to inspire others with these ideas. The ideas were terrible in their simplicity, so that he has been called 'a terrible simplifier'. They were always likely to lead to disaster and the only surprise must be that it took so long for the disaster to become apparent. Thus it came about that Hitler, in many ways a ludicrous figure, whose capacity for evil was usually underestimated by those who had to confront him, overshadows the whole of modern German history. It is a fact which many Germans find it difficult, even now, to come to terms with and continue to feel uneasy about. Hitler was a consummate actor. The rabble-rousing speeches of his early days were carefully rehearsed. The rages with which in his days as the Dictator he cowed even his own generals could be turned on and off to order. He could also be very charming, and combined with his excellent memory, this could make him very persuasive. He despised book-learning and treated knowledge simply as a means to an end. He was so dominating that none of the other Nazi leaders ever challenged him, even when he was plainly leading them to ruin.

The other major Nazi leaders surrounding Hitler often struck contemporaries as a group of gangsters who had made it big. There were many disreputable figures especially among the regional leaders, the *Gauleiter*, whose personal loyalty to Hitler was essential in holding the regime together. Some would, in more normal times, have been found on the inside of gaols. The three most important men in the Third Reich apart from Hitler were Göring, Goebbels and Himmler.

Hermann Göring

Hermann Göring, born in 1893, was a much decorated air ace in the First World War and his adhesion to the Nazi Party in the early 1920s was a big catch for Hitler. In the 1930s he became the second man in the Third Reich, combining in his hands a large number of important positions, and he was Hitler's designated successor. He acquired some personal popularity, for there was about him, a large fat man, a certain sense of good humour and enjoyment. He was regarded with amusement for the large number of different uniforms and outfits in which he appeared. In fact he was utterly ruthless and untouched by any moral scruples and Hitler admired him for that, calling him 'ice-cold' in a crisis. He was also very corrupt, amassing a huge trove of art treasures stolen from all over Europe. Beginning with the failure of his air force in the Battle of Britain, he rapidly lost influence. Having always been a drug addict he withdrew into a voluptuary life-style. Even at the height of his influence he was unable to stand up to Hitler.

Joseph Goebbels

Joseph Goebbels, born in 1897, was the intellectual among the Nazi leaders. He was a small, saturnine man with a club-foot and his unprepossessing appearance gave him a chip on his shoulder. He had a university education, but like many young men in the 1920s he was thoroughly foot-loose. He thought of himself as a total revolutionary set to uproot a society which he despised. He could as easily have turned to the extreme left as he did to the extreme right. In Hitler he saw and admired the greatest of revolutionaries and from the time he met him in 1926 became completely dedicated to him. As Gauleiter of Berlin in the years before 1933 he fought a no-holds-barred battle for this stronghold of the left. As propaganda chief of the Third Reich he built up the Hitler myth, the faith that held the whole ramshackle enterprise together. To this day his name is a byword for propaganda that bears little relationship to the truth. In spite of the debt Hitler owed him, Goebbels was, for a time, out of favour. He came into his own again in the latter days of the war, when the regime was most radicalised. He toured the bombed German cities, calling for total war and revenge, when Hitler himself had withdrawn from the contact with the masses which he had cultivated in his heyday. In 1945 Goebbels, seen by many as the most evil spirit of the Third Reich, chose to commit suicide by the side of his master in the Berlin bunker, having first, with his wife, killed their six children.

Heinrich Himmler

Heinrich Himmler, born in 1900, came from a conventional middle-class background. His father was a very strait-laced professor at one of Munich's leading grammar schools and also tutored some of the princes of the Bavarian royal family. He was something of a black sheep in his family, working as a chicken farmer in the Bavarian countryside. Himmler had what psychologists call an authoritarian personality and felt insecure when confronted with any kind of non-conformist behaviour. He was unimpressive in appearance, not at all like the Aryan superman he sought to breed, more like a cranky schoolmaster. Yet he became what has been called the Grand Inquisitor of the Third Reich, who enforced with relentless severity the true doctrine. He had a literal belief in the most bizarre aspects of the Nazi racial nonsense. Recruits to the SS were subjected to a minute examination of their ancestry before being accepted and the same procedure was followed for their intended brides. Himmler spent a great deal of effort through his SS organisations in chasing remains of alleged ancient Germanic cults. He took the Nazi slogan that the race was rooted in 'blood and soil' with deadly seriousness. He exhibited in his person the double-edged nature of National Socialism, on the one hand looking back to a mythical past in neurotic fear of modernity, on the other hand using the most modern methods of terrorising, exploiting and killing people. Himmler lived in great dependence on Hitler and experienced symptoms of illness if he thought anything met with the Führer's disapproval. Yet he was also a master of the power game. From small beginnings he built up a vast empire of terror, persecution and exploitation. All attempts to impose some kind of legal control over the activities of the SS, the Gestapo and the concentration camps, were successfully warded off, for they were always covered by orders of the Führer. Towards the end of the war, when Himmler's power was at its peak, he was looking for a way out, but could not bring himself until the very last minute to break the bond that held him to the Führer. Himmler was a truly sinister figure, bearing out with his colourless personality the banality of evil.

4 The First World War and Revolution

The Outbreak of War

In the crisis following the assassination of the Austrian heir to the throne, Archduke Ferdinand, and his wife, at Sarajevo on 28 June 1914 Bethmann Hollweg hoped, by fully backing Austria-Hungary, to achieve a weakening of the Triple Entente of Russia, France and Britain. It was a high-risk strategy which failed. In the final stages of the crisis the plans of the military for mobilisation, as well as the public emotions aroused, deprived the diplomats of the chance to work out another compromise, as had been done in previous crises. The European power system went out of control and lurched into war. Bethmann Hollweg achieved, however, one important success. The German public became convinced that Russia was the principal aggressor. To the German labour movement, reactionary Tsarist Russia had always been a bugbear. Fear of Russia was, therefore, a chief factor in inducing the SPD to give the German entry into war their backing. Great efforts had been made by the Second International, the liaison body for the socialist parties of the various countries, to avert war. When it came to the crunch, however, these parties, in spite of their long-standing professions of workers' solidarity across the nations, mostly supported the stand of their own nations. Nationality proved, contrary to Marxist predictions, more potent than class.

This was certainly true of the German socialists. Without the collaboration of the labour movement it would hardly have been possible for Germany to fight a total war for four years. It was, therefore, a decisive moment when on 4 August 1914 the SPD voted for the war credits, the initial extra money required for the war, in the Reichstag. The deep divisions of the previous year seemed to be over. This moment of national unity, of an enthusiastic uprising to defend the Fatherland against its enemies, made a deep impression on nationally-minded Germans. The spirit of August 1914 was recalled frequently later on, not least by the Nazis with their emphasis on *Volksgemeinschaft*, the community of the *Volk* (people). For the moment all political controversy ceased and a *Burgfrieden* (peace within the castle) was declared.

The Course of the War till 1916

German war plans were based on a rapid defeat of France, to be followed by a turn eastwards to beat Russia. This was the Schlieffen Plan, which had in the final stages of the July crisis, made the generals force the hands of the politicians in ordering a rapid mobilisation. It involved moving the German right wing through Belgium, thus making British entry into the war all but inevitable. By September 1914, when the French managed to halt the German enveloping movement around Paris at the Battle of the Marne, the Schlieffen Plan had failed. The result was the static trench warfare of the Western front, which exacted an enormous price in casualties. It was a war of attrition in which Germany's inferior resources would ultimately tell against her.

On the German home front the *Burgfrieden* soon began to fray at the edges. A significant minority in the SPD had opposed the war from the beginning and, as the hardships suffered by the ordinary people grew, the voice of the anti-war faction became louder. The leaders of the party could only justify their support for the war if it was fought for just ends, democratic reform at home and a just and durable peace without annexations abroad. On the other side of the political divide views moved in the opposite direction. The nationalist section of opinion felt that only far-reaching acquisitions of territory could secure the raw materials and markets to make Germany a world power. Politicians, publicists, university professors and others vied with each other in demanding annexations of territory and resources in Western and Eastern Europe. This annexationism, as it came to be called, was also connected with the pre-war domestic political controversies. The annexationists felt that only a victorious peace with its rewards in booty could maintain the power structure of Imperial Germany and the privileges of its ruling classes. As the prospect of a swift German victory receded, the war aims of the annexationists escalated, for only in this way could the great sacrifices and casualties be justified, something of a paradox. Instead of the war being fought for a limited end, the war itself and its insatiable appetite for lives and goods dictated ever more ambitious ends.

There was also a wide-spread feeling that Germany deserved to win because of the superiority of her culture. It was arrogantly claimed that German thought was more profound than the shallow rationalism of the French, German values higher and more heroic than the materialism and commercialism of the British, and German civilisation altogether more advanced and enlightened than that of the barbaric benighted Russians.

The Hindenburg-Ludendorff Partnership Takes Over in 1916

While the German offensive had ground to a halt on the Marne in September 1914, Hindenburg, with Ludendorff as his Chief of Staff (see pages 13-14), had successfully stopped the Russian advance into East Prussia, the only occasion during the whole of the war when German territory had been directly threatened. The Germans virtually annihilated two Russian armies in the battles of Tannenberg and the Masurian Lakes in August and September 1914. To enable Hindenburg and Ludendorff to halt the Russian steamroller vital divisions had been diverted to them from the offensive in France, one of the reasons for its failure. Tannenberg turned Hindenburg and Ludendorff into heroes.

Falkenhayn, appointed supreme German commander after the failure of the Schlieffen Plan, still believed that the war could be won decisively only on the Western front. In 1916 he hoped to bleed the French to death in the battle of Verdun, but the fortress, a salient in the German line, survived. The British were about to make the same vain attempt to achieve a breakthrough in the Battle of the Somme, starting on 1 July 1916. Falkenhayn's failure led the German political and military establishment to look for fresh leaders to give German morale a lift. Hindenburg and Ludendorff were the obvious choice and on 29 August 1916 they were appointed Chief of the Supreme Command and Quartermaster-General respectively, 3 OHL for short, the third version of the *Oberste Heeresleitung*. They became the virtual dictators of Germany for the rest of the war. Since 1914 the Kaiser had been little more than a figurehead, though his agreement was still necessary in many matters; the Chancellor lacked, under the imperial constitution, popular or parliamentary support and could not, therefore, impose his will.

The situation in Germany differed markedly from the despised western democracies. In Britain and France strong politicians with a popular base, Lloyd George and Clemenceau, came to the fore, who would eventually bring the war to a victorious conclusion. In Germany the military had become totally dominant and could enforce policies that were politically disastrous. It was a dictatorship limited only by the fact that without popular backing and the collaboration of the trade union and SPD leaders the war could not continue. The major decisions which 3 OHL took in the next eighteen months in pursuit of total war all proved in the end counterproductive and brought about Germany's defeat.

The German Home Front in Mid-war

It will never be possible to be entirely certain to what extent the SPD's support for the war in 1914 was really representative of working-class opinion. It has to be remembered that the SPD, with about a million members in 1914, and the trade unions, with about two and a half million, comprised only a minority of the total German working class. What is certain is that the initial enthusiasm for war, which may have left the leaders of the labour movement no option but to support it, soon faded. Germany was in fact less well prepared for the huge upheavals entailed by war than liberal Britain. Initially, there was a big upsurge of unemployment, causing great hardship. This was soon replaced by a labour shortage, bringing women, young persons and unskilled workers often from rural areas into the factories. Many of these new workers had to labour to exhaustion to keep the munitions and armaments flowing. In spite of all official efforts wages did not keep up with prices and a black market in basic foodstuffs emerged, in which the length of a person's purse counted. This also affected many middle-class groups, civil servants, white-collar workers, small businessmen. Small businesses, in branches not connected with the war effort, were closed down. Big business producing for war did well and its profits swelled. The inequalities of sacrifice caused huge resentment, showing itself in local food riots, often led by women. For the time being such protests had little political edge. At least until 1917 there was a sharp decline in trade union membership and war-time conditions had led, as in Britain, to a virtual standstill in local party politics. Anti-war movements were vigorously suppressed by the authorities. The country was divided into military districts, in which generals exercised far-reaching powers of censorship and control under a law of siege dating back to the nineteenth century.

Divisions within the SPD

The line taken by the SPD and trade union leaders in supporting the war was therefore not seriously challenged for the first year or two after August 1914. To these leaders the pro-war stance made sense. They, and for the time being most of their followers, believed that the future well-being of the German working class was tied to a German victory. They also saw that with the outbreak of war the doors of the political and military leaders were open to them. They were no longer political outcasts. They hoped that political reforms, such as the abolition of the Prussian three-tier franchise, would inevitably come. Essentially this was the outlook that shaped the course of the SPD and trade union leaders right through the revolution of 1918/19. There had, however, been a sizeable minority which even in August 1914 stuck to the party line with reluctance. Soon a number of SPD Reichstag deputies, among whom Karl Liebknecht was the most radical, ceased to support the periodical votes required for war credits. In the SPD before the war Liebknecht and Rosa Luxemburg had been the leaders of the extreme left, which remained committed to revolution, and they now led the anti-war movement. They had a numerically small organisation called the Spartakus League, eventually the nucleus of the German Communist Party. Soon others, not necessarily on the left, joined the opposition to the war, because they felt that the claim that Germany was fighting a defensive war was false in the first place, and that annexationism was now so rampant that it deprived the war of its moral justification. By March 1916 the anti-war group formed an organisation and a year later they set up a separate party, the USPD (Independent SPD). It had little unity and only opposition to the war kept it together. When these changes at the top of

the party were added to the growing unrest among the rank and file in 1917, a significant anti-war movement within Germany had arisen.

1917: A Year of Decision

In spite of increasing disaffection on the home front, the Hindenburg-Ludendorff leadership still enjoyed great confidence among the mass of the German population. By the end of 1916 the military leaders were able to impose their view that the German submarine fleet should sink ships on sight, regardless of the risk that this was likely to bring the United States into the war. Once again, as in the case of the Schlieffen Plan, narrowly logistic calculations proved wrong and politically disastrous. German decision-makers, blinded by their ideology of German superiority, grossly underestimated the United States, as they had done Britain.

The entry of the United States into the war against Germany was decisive in the long run, but immediately events in Russia had a more direct impact. In March 1917 the Tsar was toppled and the succeeding Russian governments found it increasingly difficult to maintain their policy of continuing the war on the side of the Allies. The German High Command speeded the disintegration of Russia by facilitating the transport of Lenin and a group of revolutionaries from their Swiss exile to St Petersburg, where they arrived in April 1917. This so-called 'sealed train' episode, because the revolutionaries were not allowed to leave their train while it was crossing German territory, again shows 3 OHL in the relentless short-term pursuit of total war, heedless of long-term consequences. Hindenburg and Ludendorff had also pressed the implementation of total mobilisation of the home front. The Auxiliary Labour Law of December 1916 permitted the conscription of all men between the ages of

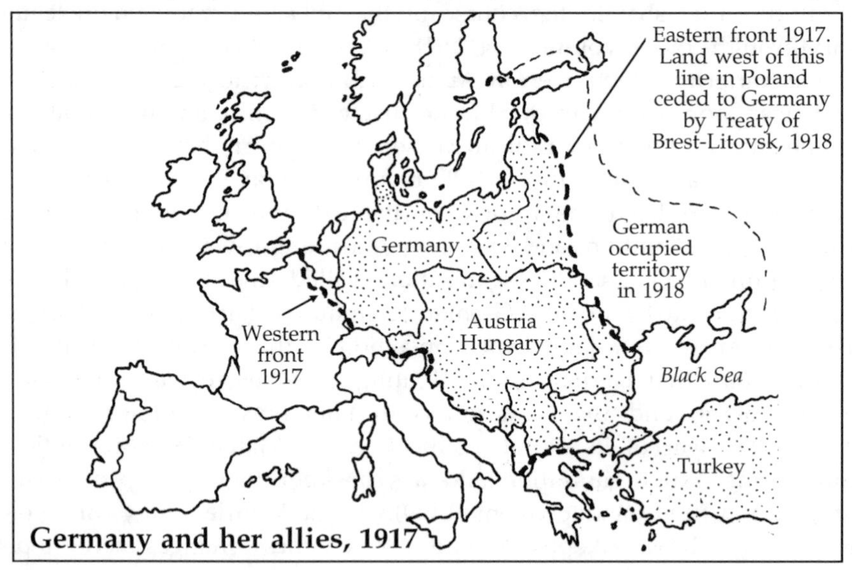

Germany and her allies, 1917

17 and 61. To make this draconian measure acceptable considerable concessions had to be made to the trade unions, which were given greater legal recognition than they had ever had. In enterprises employing more than fifty persons councils with workers' representatives were established. The official leaders of the trade unions and of the SPD felt confirmed in their view that they were no longer outsiders and that a share of power and a large measure of reform would inevitably come when the war was over. This increased the mistrust between the leaders of the labour movement and the rank and file progressively disenchanted by the war.

The Fall of Bethmann Hollweg

In the meantime Bethmann Hollweg, gravely weakened though he was by the rise of the virtual dictatorship of Hindenburg and Ludendorff, was promoting promises of post-war reforms to maintain the morale of the masses. In April 1917 the Emperor, in his Easter message, made a guarded commitment to the reform of the Prussian three-tier franchise. The parties in the Reichstag were now also on the move, having hitherto more or less stuck to the low-key role allotted to them under the *Burgfrieden.* They formed an Inter-Party Committee, representing most of the parties other than those on the right, and began to discuss the terms of a peace resolution, the basis on which a peace might be negotiated. In a somewhat contradictory way some of the party leaders were also sympathetic to the determined attempts of Ludendorff to get rid of Bethmann Hollweg. On 13 July the Chancellor resigned and on 19 July a resolution, demanding peace without annexations, passed the Reichstag.

The parties collaborating in the Inter-Party Committee were unable and unwilling to appoint Bethmann Hollweg's successor. At this critical juncture in Germany's affair Michaelis, a colourless and obscure civil servant, was appointed Chancellor by the Emperor. He accepted the peace resolution with the proviso 'as I interpret it', thereby rendering it meaningless. Michaelis lasted only three months and was succeeded by Count Hertling, an elderly and ailing Bavarian politician belonging to the Catholic Centre Party.

Towards the Last Push

By the autumn of 1917 Germany's situation could be interpreted in two starkly contrasting ways. Either it was a matter of seeking a compromise peace before it was too late, or a final all-out push could still secure victory for the German armies. The Reichstag's peace resolution, ineffective as it proved to be, was clearly pointing in the first direction. The SPD leaders were well aware how fragile the morale of the masses had become and that it, and with it their own hold on their followers, might break if willingness to negotiate a reasonable peace as soon as possible was not demonstrated. Germany would follow Russia into revolution. There were many indications that the time was more ripe for compromise than ever before.

Russia's will to fight was waning and even in France and Britain there were voices asking for negotiations. There was a peace initiative by the Pope and an international meeting of socialist parties in Stockholm. The Austrians, near the end of their tether, were secretly promoting peace feelers. It is impossible now to know if an end to the war could have been negotiated in 1917 if the will to do so had prevailed in Germany. Even in the Allied countries, despite many discouraging setbacks, the view was still in the ascendant that the war could be won outright and that to contemplate any other outcome was virtual treason. This was the view that certainly predominated in Germany and it was powerfully reinforced when, after the Bolshevik Revolution of November 1917, Russia sued for peace. At last the two-front war was over and Germany could concentrate all her forces to achieve a breakthrough in the West. This was Ludendorff's chosen way forward and it prevailed.

The German High Command's position was underpinned by a campaign of indoctrination and mass mobilisation that counterbalanced the doubts of the parties in the Reichstag and the signs of exhaustion among the population at large. With the support of Ludendorff the Fatherland Party was launched in the autumn of 1917. It was not a party in the electoral sense but a propaganda campaign which by 1918 had enlisted over a million members, more than the SPD at its peak. It has been called the greatest mass mobilisation of chauvinism before National Socialism. There was an educational programme, also in the army, to counteract weaknesses of morale and stress the need for a *Siegfrieden,* a peace based on total victory.

Separate Peace in the East and Last Offensive in the West

The peace negotiations with the Russian Bolshevik Government could have been used by Germany as part of a general move towards a negotiated peace, but this was not what Ludendorff and those who thought like him had in mind. They now saw an opportunity to create the vast empire in the East that would give Germany a secure source of foodstuffs and raw materials. With the Russian armies disintegrating Lenin and his colleagues thought they had only one card left to play against Germany, the threat of revolution spreading throughout Europe. In the end Lenin, Trotsky and their associates had no alternative but to sign, in March 1918, the humiliating terms of the Treaty of Brest-Litovsk, which created a band of German satellite states from the Baltic through Poland to the Ukraine. The lure of victory and conquest was still so strong even in the SPD that, in spite of its declared opposition to annexations, it could not vote against the Treaty, when it came before the Reichstag, and abstained. The Germans, however, hardly obtained from this Treaty what they had hoped. They still had to leave large numbers of troops to police the vast area and only disappointing quantities of grain could be extracted from the Ukraine, the potential granary. The severe terms imposed at Brest-Litovsk strengthened the determination in the West to fight to a finish.

In the meantime there were further signs that morale on the German home front was weakening. In January 1918 there was a big wave of strikes in the major industrial centres, particularly Berlin, led by left-wingers opposed to the war. The authorities repressed the strikes, in many cases sending ringleaders to the front. In the meantime 3 OHL, disregarding all danger signals, went ahead with the preparations for an offensive on the Western front that was to achieve a decisive breakthrough to the Channel. It started on 21 March and initially led to a 40 mile German advance at the junction of the British and French armies, the greatest victory on the Western front since the fronts had stabilised in 1914. The British Fifth Army was particularly hard hit and Lloyd George's Government nearly fell. As so often before, a final decision eluded the Germans. From April to June 1918 the main German thrust was shifted from one sector to another, still gaining territory, but a decisive breakthrough never came.

Ludendorff had overreached himself. There were no reserves left to maintain his front-line strength. When it became apparent that the hopes placed in his offensive had proved false, the morale of the German soldiers cracked. Increasing numbers reported sick, others went absent when going on leave. On 18 July the French, with American support, retook most of the Marne salient won by the German spring offensives. On 8 August, the 'Black Day of the German Army', the British used tanks on a large scale in their sector and moved forward towards the old Somme battlefields of 1916. These German defeats conclusively deprived Ludendorff of any possibility of recovering the strategic initiative. There was not yet a complete rout, but a gradual retreat towards the German frontiers. With fresh American troops arriving in increasing numbers, it could be only a matter of time before the Allies achieved a decisive breakthrough. The threat was aggravated by the fact that Germany's allies were about to surrender. The first actually to do so was Bulgaria, on 29 September 1918.

Ludendorff Presses for an Armistice

The German political establishment was slow to wake up to the crisis facing them. In some quarters there were still discussions about how to divide up the booty expected in the East and which German prince might ascend the throne of the German Polish puppet state. If even the political leaders had so little inkling of the catastrophe about to engulf them, it may be imagined how deep was the shock to the general public, fed on a propaganda diet of constant victory since 1914, when they found defeat staring them in the face. In all that follows this suddenness with which the realisation of defeat struck the Germans as a nation must be borne in mind. It was Ludendorff, the champion of all-out victory, who, under the impact of Bulgaria's defection, took the decisive step in asking for an armistice. To make such a request credible, it was necessary to install a government that

Document. Ludendorff tells his staff about the request for an armistice, 29 September 1918.

I have advised His Majesty to bring those groups into the government whom we have in the main to thank for the fact that matters have reached this pass. We will therefore now see these gentlemen move into the ministries. Let them now conclude the peace that has to be negotiated. Let them eat the broth they have cooked for us.

---

would be representative of the parties in the Reichstag. For Hindenburg and Ludendorff this was also a way of shifting the blame for defeat on to the shoulders of the civilian politicians, an aim in which they were only too successful. The ground was prepared for the myth, later to be known as 'the stab in the back', that the German army was not defeated on the battlefield, but subverted on the home front. On 29 September a meeting in the presence of the Kaiser decided that a new chancellor should be appointed, who would take into his government representatives of the political parties in the Reichstag, including the SPD. His first task would be to request President Wilson of the United States to arrange an armistice. Even now the choice of the chancellor was the Emperor's and it fell on Prince Max of Baden, the heir to the throne of Germany's most liberal state, but hardly the man for this supreme crisis.

When the full extent of Germany's military disaster was revealed to the party leaders they were stunned. With the patriotic sense that had marked their conduct since 1914, the leaders of the SPD decided to take up the poisoned chalice now offered them and participated in the new government. The key figure in this decision was Friedrich Ebert who had increasingly emerged has the most powerful man in the SPD since the death of Bebel and was to play a central role in the events about to unfold. Ludendorff forced the immediate despatch of the armistice request, against the better judgement of the new Chancellor, for the General was now fearful that a new Allied offensive would break through into Germany and that there would be nothing left but total surrender and the triumph of Bolshevism, as he saw it, in Germany. In fact the request for an armistice was a point of no return that within five weeks led to the collapse of the German monarchies and to revolution. Any credibility which the imperial system still retained in the eyes of ordinary Germans was gone. Confidence in the military leadership, still strong a few weeks earlier, turned into hatred for all things military and determination to be rid of all its manifestations. Nowhere was this feeling stronger than among the men still subject to military discipline.

Towards Revolution

President Wilson had been asked to arrange an armistice with the Allied powers on the basis of his Fourteen Points, proclaimed in the previous

January. These Fourteen Points constituted a programme for the post-war world based on self-determination of all peoples and on an international order constructed for the avoidance of war in the future. The world was to be made safe for democracy. To achieve this a League of Nations was to be established, with the power to order action by its member states against an aggressor state. The return of Alsace-Lorraine to France and the establishment of an independent Polish state with access to the sea was envisaged in the Fourteen Points. In the exchange of notes between Wilson and the German Government it soon became apparent that the President of the United States and the Allies were distrustful of the changes so far made in Germany and wanted evidence that the imperial system and its militarism was at an end and that the move towards democracy was genuine. Wilson's notes in October 1918 encouraged the already growing impatience of the German masses at the continued presence of the Kaiser himself and of the monarchy. The Kaiser was seen to stand in the way of peace and only his speedy abdication could have saved the monarchy as an institution. The changes so long demanded, full parliamentary government, an equal and universal suffrage everywhere, were implemented at the end of October, but in the headlong rush of events and still unaccompanied by the Kaiser's abdication, they were hardly noticed.

Naval Mutiny Starts Revolt

On the other hand there were still those, especially in the Army and the Navy, who were unwilling to acknowledge defeat and found the terms outlined in Wilson's notes unacceptable. Ludendorff soon changed his mind about an armistice and demanded a fight to the finish. He was dismissed, his place taken by Groener, a non-Prussian desk general, who had taken a leading part in mobilising the German home front since 1916 and was respected in the SPD and trade union world. Hindenburg remained and it was not to be the last occasion that he, the man with the image of rock-like loyalty, would throw an associate to the wolves. The leaders of the Navy also wanted to go on fighting. They saw an opportunity to retrieve their reputation, damaged by their earlier inaction. They would fight a final battle against the Royal Navy, bring relief to the Army in France and scupper the move towards an Armistice. It was the order of the admirals to the major German battleships to get up steam on 29 October that proved to be the final signal for revolution. Already in 1917 the German Navy had had a mutiny. In the confined space and tough conditions on board ship the differences between officers and men caused deep resentment. Now the German sailors refused to die in a vain attempt to avoid defeat. They disobeyed orders, hoisted the Red Flag and formed councils to control the ships and the ports and towns on Germany's seaboard. They sent delegations inland to raise the flag of revolt elsewhere. Within days workers' and soldiers' councils assumed authority in many

German cities. In the meantime the Kaiser, to escape the pressure on him to abdicate, had left Berlin and gone to General Headquarters at Spa, in Belgium. The danger to the survival of monarchy in Germany grew when on 7 November the Bavarian King was forced to leave his capital Munich. A combination of forces from the USPD and disaffected peasants had taken over the city without a fight, led by a journalist from the USPD, Kurt Eisner. The defection of Austria-Hungary ten days earlier had left Germany wide open to an attack from the South and this contributed to the outbreak of revolution in Munich. One of the oldest German monarchies had fallen and it had been shown that the forces of law and order, the Army and the bureaucracy, were now so completely demoralised and paralyzed that they could no longer put up any resistance to such a take-over.

The Kaiser's Abdication

At last, two days later, the revolutionary wave spread to Berlin. Large numbers of workers left their factories and converged on the centre of the city. Belatedly, Prince Max announced the abdication of the Kaiser, even though he had not yet got Wilhelm's approval from Spa. He handed over his own powers as Chancellor to Friedrich Ebert. Speaking from a window in the Reichstag building, Scheidemann, second-in-command to Ebert, proclaimed a republic. He acted without Ebert's approval, but his intention was to preempt the proclamation of a socialist republic, based on the councils, by the radical Karl Liebknecht. In the meantime, at Spa, the Kaiser was told by Hindenburg and Groener that any attempt by him to return to Germany at the head of the Army, to crush the revolution, was doomed. The Army would return home in good order, but it would no longer follow the Kaiser. The Kaiser was advised by his generals that for his own safety he should leave for Holland. He took their advice and ended a thousand years or more of monarchy in Germany for good. As he boarded the train he remarked: 'I am so ashamed'. It was a revolution, but what kind of revolution?

Parliamentary Democracy or Dictatorship of the Proletariat?

When Friedrich Ebert took over the chancellorship from Prince Max of Baden at noon on 9 November 1918 he was the beneficiary of a revolution that he and his party, the SPD, had neither made nor desired. They would have been quite content with what had been established by the end of October, a fully parliamentary monarchy similar to the British. They would have been quite prepared to continue, under Ebert, the coalition with the bourgeois parties in the Reichstag which had been formed under Prince Max. But the sudden German military collapse and the disillusionment of the German masses with their previous rulers had quickly moved matters much further. Ebert and his colleagues in the leadership of the SPD had now to put themselves at the head of the revolutionary movement if they were not to lose control to the USPD and to the even more radical forces around Liebknecht, Luxemburg and the Spartakus League. The Spartacists were about to form a separate party, the Communist Party of Germany (KPD). Ebert and the SPD wanted to move as rapidly as possible to the election of a constituent assembly that would confirm the parliamentary democracy already established and fill in its details. But to maintain themselves in power until such an assembly could be elected they had now to drop the coalition with the bourgeois parties and enter one with the USPD. This interim body was given the somewhat misleading title Council of People's Commissars, thus adopting the language of the Russian Revolution. Its six members were drawn equally from the SPD and the USPD. Ebert and the leader of the USPD theoretically shared the chairmanship, but the former almost immediately took the lead.

Two incompatible views of the future were barely and only temporarily reconciled: the SPD vision of consolidating the already introduced parliamentary democracy, and the view of the left that a dictatorship of the proletariat would lead to a socialist society based on the councils. In the ensuing power struggle Ebert and the SPD held all the cards. By placing the chancellorship in his hands Prince Max had ensured that the whole state apparatus, with its tens of thousands of civil servants, remained loyal to Ebert. Soon OHL also recognised the authority of Ebert. This was the meaning of the famous telephone call, on the evening of 9 November, between Groener and Ebert, in which the former undertook to bring the Army home in orderly fashion, in return for the latter's keeping the threat of a Bolshevik-type revolution at bay.

A Possible Third Way?

Contemporary observers and later historians have asked the question whether there was no alternative between the parliamentary democracy that came into being, but was eventually to end so disastrously with Hitler and the Third Reich, and a dictatorship of the proletariat on the Russian model based on soviets or councils, which, from the present-day perspective, has turned out to be equally disastrous and productive of human suffering and doomed in the long run. Some have argued for a third way, which would have laid firmer foundations for parliamentary democracy by bringing about greater social and economic changes to match the political changes. Few would now argue that a revolution on the Russian model was either desirable or even possible in a highly developed country like Germany, where male workers had had the vote for half a century and where a dictatorship of the proletariat would, therefore, have been a retrogressive development. To this extent the course of history has justified the line taken by Ebert and the SPD.

Failure to Control the Military

Nevertheless, Ebert and his colleagues have been criticised for being too preoccupied with maintaining order, too trustful of the civil servants and military leaders inherited from the discredited imperial regime, and too fearful of the threat from the extreme left. Thereby, it is argued, they missed the opportunity of getting rid of some of the obstacles to a properly functioning democracy. Some basic industries, such as coal mining, should have been nationalised and landownership should have been reformed by creating more peasant proprietors on the big agricultural estates in the eastern provinces of Prussia. In this way some social groups, the owners of heavy industry and the Junkers, would have been weakened in their ability to obstruct the parliamentary democracy of Weimar. Such arguments need to be treated with caution, because the circumstances in which the Weimar Republic failed in the early 1930s were, as we shall see, very different from those prevailing at the end of the First World War. National Socialism became, in the circumstances of the Great Depression after 1929, a mass movement and neither some measures of nationalisation nor land reform would necessarily have prevented that. Ebert and his colleagues are most open to criticism for their failure to deal adequately with the control of military power, as a further examination of the course of the revolution will show. The leadership of the Army, the former General Staff, remained

Street poster, 1919. Peace: we will get it through order!

insufficiently subordinated to the civil power and gave the new parliamentary democracy only a conditional loyalty. This was to prove a crucial factor in the failure of Weimar after 1930. Remains of the old imperial army, mostly through specially recruited volunteer forces, so-called *Freikorps,* were used by the Ebert Government and its successors to crush uprisings from the left in 1919 and beyond. This created great bitterness among the working class in Germany's major industrial centres and provided a considerable popular base for the initially small German Communist Party. The deep division of the left was another factor eventually to facilitate the Nazi take-over.

From Revolution to Near-Civil War

Initially the German Revolution caused remarkably little bloodshed. The old imperial regime and its agents had given up without a struggle and accepted the authority of the new masters. The whole German middle class, previously nationalistic and loyal to the Kaiser, was in chastened mood. They realised that they had to co-operate with the workers and their representatives, the SPD, as had indeed already happened in the war. For a few months, until the spring of 1919, a kind of honeymoon prevailed. The parties and social groups formerly loyal to the monarchies hoped that by embracing democracy Germany would escape the worst consequences of defeat and obtain a lenient peace from the Allies.

From its relatively non-violent beginnings the German Revolution soon drifted into tension and bloodshed. Even during the war hostility to the 'loyal' SPD and trade union leaders had run deep among those elements of the labour movement represented in the USPD. The coalition of SPD and USPD made on 9 November could only thinly paper over the cracks. Nothing could stop the harder left-wing elements from regarding the SPD leaders and even the more moderate elements in the USPD as traitors to the working class, who would take any opportunity to betray the revolution. What particularly aroused the suspicion of the left was the relationship between the Ebert Government and what remained of the Army and its leaders. They feared that the troops returning from the Western front would be used against them and their efforts to push the revolution further. Ebert and his colleagues, on the other hand, were in urgent need of protection in Berlin where at any moment a mob might take over the government buildings. In fact all efforts by OHL to maintain a force, capable of preserving order, failed. The soldiers returned home in orderly fashion, but then either disappeared, or, under the influence of the soldiers' councils in the home army, refused to play any role that could be described as counterrevolutionary. Efforts by the Council of People's Commissars to recruit a reliable republican guard also failed. Not many workers were any longer willing to submit to military discipline and the divisions between right and left were so deep that such a republican force,

had it been possible to establish it, would have been in practice paralysed.

The Freikorps

These were the reasons for the recruitment of the Freikorps, volunteers organised by former officers and NCOs. Such troops were also used in the extremely confused and fluid situation on Germany's eastern borders. The Freikorps were strongly nationalistic and anti-revolutionary. Their members were men who had fought in the trenches and knew no methods other than war and violence. Some were also students, too young to have been involved in the war, but again strongly opposed to the revolutionaries, whom they saw as Bolsheviks, and fervently nationalistic. The loyalty of the Freikorps to the republic and its government was very questionable. Yet it was the republican government, which in the absence of other reliable forces, used the Freikorps against the challenge from the left reaching a peak in 1919. In many parts of Germany, where there were great concentrations of industrial workers, particularly major cities like Berlin, the Ruhr and Central Germany, there was something close to a civil war.

Elections for a Constituent Assembly

In the meantime the Ebert Government, in spite of the daily insecurity which surrounded it, was making progress towards the election of a constituent assembly that would give the new state of affairs a legal basis. On 16 December 1918 a General Congress of Workers' and Soldiers' Councils met in Berlin, elected by the councils throughout the country. The left had hoped to make this congress a launching pad for their scheme to build a socialist republic on the basis of the councils. In their view elections to a constituent assembly could only be held when the supremacy of the working class had been firmly established and great changes had been made in the social structure. In fact the Congress was dominated by the SPD, which had nearly 60 per cent of the delegates. The most prominent radical leaders, Liebknecht and Luxemburg, were not even elected to the Congress. Modern research has shown that the councils, far from being the revolutionary hotbeds the left hoped and the right feared, were outside the great cities often dominated by moderates or by the middle classes. The membership of the soldiers' councils was, owing to rapid demobilisation, very fluid. From this it can be argued that the councils could hardly have played the role as bearers of a new revolutionary order demanded by the left. On the other hand, the right need not have been quite as fearful of them as it was. Hence the claim of some historians writing after the Second World War that the Ebert Government should have used the councils as a 'democratising factor'. How this could have been done is not clear, for once a constituent assembly was elected there was no room for an alternative system of councils. The General Congress of Councils in fact endorsed Ebert's demand for a speedy election of an assembly and the elections were fixed for 19 January 1919. On the other hand, a majority of the Congress endorsed a strongly anti-militarist programme, known as the Hamburg Points, including abolition of all insignia of rank, far-reaching powers for the soldiers' councils in matters of discipline, and election of officers. Ebert had to agree to the Hamburg Points, but it soon became clear that the Army Command would not accept them and that the Government was unable and unwilling to force them to do so.

The Spartacist Rising

A fortnight before the elections the Ebert Government faced its most serious challenge from the left since it had taken office, the so-called Spartacist Rising in Berlin. By this time the USPD representatives, opposed to the handling of the security and military problems by their SPD colleagues, had left the Council of People's Commissars. The extreme left, the Spartakus League and other groups, now constituted as the Communist Party (KPD), decided on an open rising against a government, which in their eyes was betraying the revolution. Rosa Luxemburg, who believed that revolutions had to develop from a spontaneous move by the masses, was doubtful of the wisdom of the rising, but went along with it. It was crushed by Freikorps and other troops available in the Berlin area. Gustav Noske, a defence expert in the SPD and soon to be Minister of Defence, emerged as the strong man of the Ebert Government, prepared to use force unrestrainedly against this and future uprisings from the left. He was prepared to trust the generals in charge of what was left of the regular army, now called Reichswehr, and the Freikorps. After the crushing of the Spartacist rising Liebknecht and Luxemburg were arrested and murdered on their way to prison, on 15 January 1919. Their deaths, at the hands of soldiers enlisted to protect an SPD government, deepened the divisions in the German working class and left wounds which never completely healed throughout the Weimar period.

Questions to Consider. A Possible Third Way?

- Was there an alternative third way, between a dictatorship of the proletariat on the Russian model, and a parliamentary democracy on the Western model?
- Would such a third way have provided better conditions for Weimar democracy?
- Could workers' and soldiers' councils have been used to give firmer foundations for democracy in Germany?
- Would measures such as the nationalisation of coal mines or the break-up of the great landed estates in the eastern provinces have weakened the anti-democratic, anti-republican forces?
- Did the Ebert Government rely too much on military forces, such as the Freikorps, not loyal to the republic, and what alternatives were there?

5 The Weimar Republic

The Constituent Assembly

The hostilities between the SPD and the radical left were detrimental to the long-term health of German democracy, but they could not stop the confirmation of the parliamentary democracy envisaged by the SPD leaders and at this stage welcomed by most of the population. The elections of 19 January were contested by essentially the same political parties that had already existed in the imperial era. The left was represented by the SPD and the USPD, the recently founded KPD having decided to boycott the elections. The left-wing liberals, or Progressives, now called themselves German Democratic Party (DDP, *Deutsche Demokratische Partei*). Having already collaborated with the SPD in the Interparty Committee of 1917, they saw the future of the parliamentary democracy based on a collaboration between the progressive sections of the middle class and the working class. Even now it proved impossible to unite all liberals in one party and a right-wing liberal party, the successors of the National Liberals, also entered the lists under the misleading name of German People's Party (DVP, *Deutsche Volkspartei*). It soon became the preferred vehicle of industry and business, but under the leadership of Stresemann it distanced itself from a restoration of the monarchy and accepted the republic in due course. On the right the old nationalist and conservative parties reappeared as the German National People's Party (DNVP, *Deutschnationale Volkspartei*). They made a bow towards democracy by calling themselves a people's party. Under the wing of the DNVP there sheltered initially all the nationalist, racialist and anti-Semitic extremists, many of whom were later to join the Nazis. Last, but not least, there was still the Catholic Centre Party (*Zentrum*), though its Bavarian wing was shortly to turn itself into a separate but not competing party, the Bavarian People's Party (BVP, *Bayerische Volkspartei*). Essentially it was, and remained until the rise of the Nazis into a mass party after 1929, a six-party system, two socialist, two liberal, one conservative and one catholic party. Prominent among the weaknesses blamed on the Weimar Republic was that its proportional representation system encouraged too many parties, no less than thirty-six according to later Nazi propaganda. It is true that there were a lot of minor parties in some elections of the Weimar period, but they were only occasionally of any real importance. Even with six major parties, however, coalition government is all but inevitable. A first-past-the-post electoral system tending towards a two-party situation, such as the British, could not have been introduced in Germany in 1918, because the parties surviving from the imperial period would not have accepted it.

Table 5.1. Constituent Assembly elections, 19 January 1919 (per cent)

Party	Per cent
USPD	7.6
SPD	37.9
DDP	18.6
DVP	4.4
Z+BVP	19.7
DNVP	10.3

It can be seen that the radical left was numerically quite weak, in spite of all the stir it was causing in Berlin and some other great urban centres. In the light of these figures it is difficult to believe that a revolution based on the councils could have been successful. There is, therefore, much in the argument, advanced by defenders of the SPD, that the uprisings of the extreme left played into the hands of those on the right, who never wanted a democracy. Although the SPD emerged as much the largest party, showing that the rank and file workers did not at this stage share the divisions among their leaders, even the two socialist parties together did not have a majority. Therefore the vision of a parliamentary regime based on the collaboration between the SPD, the liberals and the Centre Party, foreshadowed since 1917, had to become a reality. It should also be noted that at this stage more than three-quarters of the electorate voted for the three clearly democratic parties, SPD, Centre and DDP. Unfortunately, this degree of support for democracy soon declined steeply.

The Weimar Constitution

After the elections the Council of People's Commissars disappeared and a coalition government of SPD, DDP and Centre was formed under Scheidemann. Ebert became the interim President of the republic and was confirmed in this office once the Constitution came into full operation in August 1919. Because the situation in Berlin was too insecure, the Constituent Assembly met in the small central German town of Weimar, famous as the home of Germany's greatest writers, Goethe and Schiller, more than a century earlier. The work on the constitution, already begun before the elections, made few headlines, for its essentials were in place even before the fall of the monarchies. A few salient features of the Weimar Constitution must be mentioned here. Its supreme organ was the Reichstag, to be elected by all men and women over 21 by strict proportional representation. This widened franchise had already applied to the elections of January 1919. The government had to have the confidence of the Reichstag.

- The Weimar Constitution

The Reich President

The Reichstag was counterbalanced by a President of the Reich, who was also elected by the whole electorate. If in a first ballot no candidate received more than half the votes, there had to be a second ballot, in which new candidates could stand and in which the candidate receiving the most votes, even if it was less than 50 per cent, would be declared elected. This system was used for the first time in 1925, after the death of Ebert, and the imperial Field Marshal Hindenburg emerged as the winner on the second ballot. If there was an emergency the president could, under article 48 of the constitution, issue decrees with the force of law, provided the Reichstag did not declare them invalid (see pages 70-1). This power was very widely interpreted even by Ebert, who issued decrees to cope with the devastating inflation of 1923 (see pages 56-7), but with the intention of restoring as soon as possible the democratic process. It became even more important when from 1930 Hindenburg bypassed the Reichstag more permanently by appointing a number of chancellors whom he permitted to use his article 48 powers. The last of these chancellors was Hitler.

The Referendum and Federal Structure

Another important feature of the constitution was a provision for the holding of referenda. On paper this was a very democratic idea, but in practice it was abused by anti-democratic rabble-rousers like Hitler. Under the Weimar Constitution Germany remained a federation of states and much power continued to be exercised by the separate state governments. In the disturbed state of Weimar politics it proved particularly important that the police, and therefore the maintenance of law and order, was in the hands of the state governments, not of the Reich. Ironically the Prussian Government was now the staunchest support for the republic. It was democratically elected by universal suffrage when previously it had been, owing to the three-tier franchise, a bastion of reaction. Until 1932 it was controlled almost continuously by the same coalition (SPD, Centre and DDP), that took over in the Reich in January 1919 but was short-lived there. When the SPD-led Prussian coalition government was chased from office in July 1932 the way was finally open for the Nazi take-over. Whatever the weaknesses of the Weimar Republic, the case of Prussia shows that its failure was not inevitable.

Basic Rights

The Weimar Constitution contained a second part, concerned with the basic rights and duties of citizens, more extensive and specific than such charters usually are. Not only were equality before the law and the basic freedoms, such as freedom of speech and of religion, fully guaranteed. There was also explicit mention of all kinds of social rights, the right to work, including

Document. The Weimar Constitution

Article 161. For the maintenance of health and ability to work, for the protection of motherhood and as a provision against the economic consequences of age, weakness and the accidents of life the Reich will create a comprehensive system of insurance with the active participation of the insured.

---

provision for the unemployed, adequate protection for all human conditions from childhood, through motherhood to old age. Illegitimate children were to have the same rights of development as legitimate ones, an advanced idea for the period. Although the Ebert Government failed to carry out any of the programmes of nationalisation under discussion after the revolution, the Constitution provided for works councils on which employers and workers were to be equally represented. A Works Council Law was passed in 1920 to give effect to this paragraph of the constitution, but it failed to satisfy the far-reaching expectations of the workers. Altogether the constitution aroused expectations of social advances which would prove difficult to satisfy in a country in the reduced state of defeated Germany. The most important social achievement of the revolution in the eyes of the labour movement had been the eight-hour day. This was agreed in principle by a committee of employers and unions (*Zentralarbeitsgemeinschaft*, ZAG for short) set up in November 1918, which was intended to institutionalise the collaboration between capital and labour. As the employers regained their self-confidence, the ZAG became less important and entitlement to the eight-hour day was whittled down. Nevertheless, the Weimar Republic was founded on the hope of a more progressive democratic society than had ever before existed in Germany and which was in many respects ahead of its time.

The Weimar Constitution

- Proportional Representation in some form was inevitable, since at least six major parties existed.
- The specific form of PR in the Weimar Republic cut the link between the member and his constituency and gave great power to the party caucus compiling party lists for elections.
- There was no barrier to the rise or fall of parties. The Nazi Party is the most obvious example of rapid rise, from one election to another.
- Article 48 was needed to cope with emergencies in a crisis-ridden country, but was stretched to provide an alternative to parliamentary government.
- The Weimar Constitution includes a blueprint for an advanced social programme and helped to create expectations difficult to fulfil in a war-damaged economy.
- The basis of Weimar politics lay in co-operation between moderate

Document. The Treaty of Versailles. Article 231. (War guilt clause)
The Allied and Associated Governments declare, and Germany acknowledges, that Germany and her allies are as perpetrators responsible for all the losses and damages suffered by the Allied and Associated Governments and their citizens, as a result of the war forced upon them by the attack of Germany and her allies.

---

socialists (SPD) and the middle-class parties (DDP, DVP and Catholic Centre).

- The SPD, collaborating as a governing party with the middle-class parties, made a division between it and the radical left, opposed to the republic, inevitable.
- Weak and short-lived coalitions were the result of all these circumstances. In addition the parties were more concerned to preserve their ideological purity, rather than provide strong government, which had not been their job in Imperial Germany.
- The weakness of government in the Weimar period was overstated by those who were in principle opposed to parliamentary democracy.

The Treaty of Versailles

The German Government was not able to negotiate directly at the peace conference at Versailles. The divisions between the Allies were sufficiently serious to make it prudent to find a common position first and then present it to the Germans. This was done in May 1919. When the terms became known to the German public there was a huge outcry and a sense of betrayal. Unrealistically the German public had believed that reliance on the Fourteen Points would mean a lenient peace. There was now a mood in all parties to reject the terms, even if this would mean a resumption of hostilities under conditions hopeless for the Germans. The fact that the terms were not negotiated with Germany, but presented to her, more or less on a take-it-or-leave-it basis, meant that the treaty was considered a 'Diktat', a dictated peace. Thereafter German newspapers and publications hardly ever referred to Versailles other than as a 'Diktat', with the implication that it was not morally binding.

Ancient wisdom has it that a vanquished enemy should either be treated so leniently that the hatchet is buried for ever, or he should be so completely crushed that he can never rise again. From this point of view Versailles fell between two stools. The terms were undoubtedly very onerous for Germany and could in no way be described as conciliatory. In the circumstances this was all but inevitable. Peace could not now be made on the cold calculation of a balance of power, as in the nineteenth century. Enormous emotions had been aroused and all over the world public opinion wanted justice, revenge and an outlawing of war for ever. Several clauses of the treaty were particularly resented in Germany as a slight on her honour. This was, above all, the case with article 231, the so-called war-guilt clause, which held Germany responsible for the losses and damage caused to the Allies by her aggression. This was interpreted by the Germans as pinning the sole guilt for the outbreak of war upon them. For the Allies it supplied the moral justification for the reparations to be exacted from Germany.

Losses of Territory

The major territorial losses were Alsace-Lorraine, which many Germans had come to expect, and the Polish Corridor, separating East Prussia from the rest of the country, a loss which was never accepted as final in Germany. The German territorial losses were justified by the Allies on the principle of the self-determination of peoples, but the same principle was not applied to Austria. In spite of the expressed wish of the Austrians, shorn of their empire, to join Germany, this *Anschluss* was barred by the treaty. One can here see plainly the dilemma in which the peace-makers at Versailles found themselves. Had the Allies applied the principle of self-determination in the case of Austria, Germany would have emerged from her defeat with a territory and population larger than they were in 1914. As it was, the territory ceded amounted to a seventh of her pre-war size. Also lost were half her iron ore and a quarter of her coal production and nearly 15 per cent of her arable land. She also had to surrender much of her merchant navy and substantial amounts of rolling stock. A large part of her current coal production was mortgaged to the Allies. A final

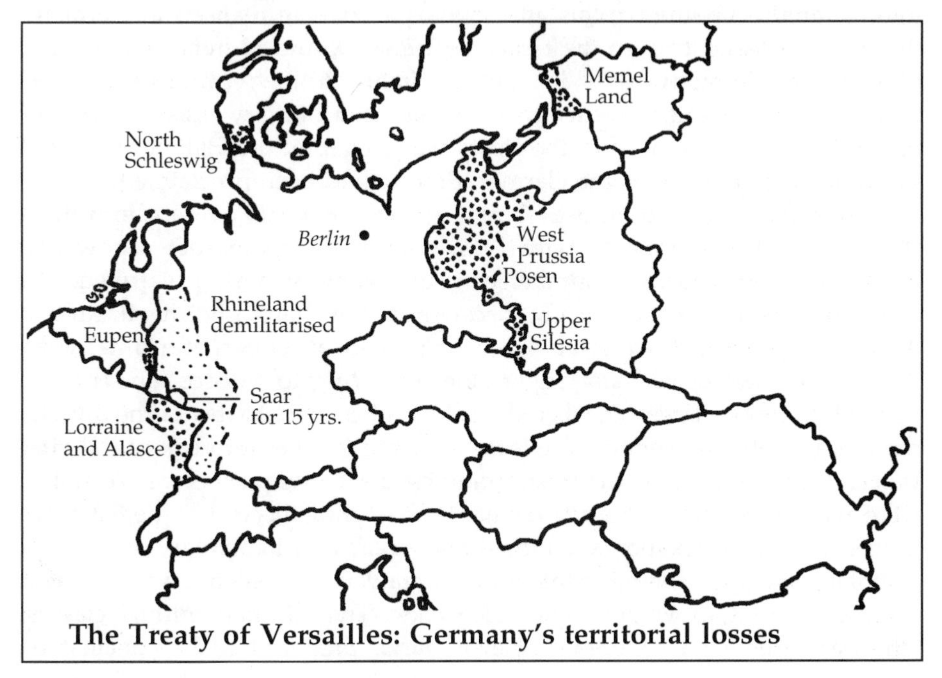

The Treaty of Versailles: Germany's territorial losses

reparations bill was not fixed in the treaty itself but was to be subsequently determined by a commission. The reparations question proved the most economically damaging legacy left by Versailles. It poisoned international relations until payments were finally suspended in 1932. Since reparations can only be obtained from a country if it is allowed to run an export surplus, the whole concept of reparations was deeply flawed and became one of the causes of the Great Depression into which the whole international economy was plunged after 1929. Also strongly resented in Germany was the loss of all her colonies, with the implication that Germans were not fit to be a colonial power. The demand for the surrender of war criminals, including the Kaiser, whom Holland refused to surrender anyway, met with a point-blank refusal. Another important section of the treaty put limits on German armaments. The most important of these limitations was that the German Army was not to exceed a total of 100,000 men and that conscription was to be barred.

Consequences of Versailles

Amidst all the outcry the treaty provoked in Germany it was almost forgotten that it left the German nation state, which was less than half a century old, intact. The French and much other opinion had wanted to divide Germany again into her constituent parts. The British and American Governments felt that only the continued existence of Germany as a state would form a barrier against the westward spread of Bolshevism. Germany was also required as a trading partner, if there was to be a recovery of the international economy. It was after agonising debate realised in Germany that if she refused to sign the treaty hostilities would be renewed and the division of Germany would then inevitably follow. Hindenburg and Groener finally brought themselves to admit that military resistance would be hopeless. On 28 June 1918 the treaty was signed in the Hall of Mirrors at Versailles where, in 1871, the German Empire had been proclaimed.

Versailles did not crush Germany and left her in an improved strategic position compared with 1914. On her eastern border a powerful Russia was replaced by a number of relatively weak states. If driven to a choice these states would turn to Germany rather than to Bolshevik Russia. All these possibilities were later to be exploited by Hitler, at a time when Britain and France were no longer able or willing to enforce the terms of Versailles. Immediately the brunt of Versailles had to be borne by the republican politicians who were least to blame for the outbreak of the First World War. In German domestic politics the consequences of Versailles were wholly negative. All the elements that until the eve of defeat were ranged behind annexationism abroad and against parliamentary democracy at home, and who had retreated into paralysis and silence when defeat became obvious, now got their voice back. The German middle classes, who had been in a sobered frame of mind, prepared to be conciliatory towards their own working classes and ready to give parliamentary government a try, now tended to turn back to their previous attitudes. It was the worst possible beginning for the Weimar Republic, about to be formally inaugurated.

Germans and the Treaty of Versailles

- Versailles was regarded in Germany as a dictated peace (Diktat), therefore not morally binding.
- The war guilt clause was seen as unjust and humiliating.
- Reparations were difficult to enforce and damaging to the world economy. They kept on reopening old wounds until finally scrapped in 1932.
- Versailles weakened Germany only temporarily. The state established by Bismarck survived intact.
- French expectations were disappointed, because Britain and USA did not conclude the promised security treaty with France.

A 1919 poster. Women. Equal rights - equal responsibilities. Vote SPD

Left-wing Uprisings

Events throughout the year 1919 were in fact eroding support for the republic, which had seemed so strong in the elections of January, not only on the right but also on the left. Among the German working class the results of the Revolution, which had been so often painted to them, in the pre-war language of the SPD, as a brightly lit upland, provoked deep disillusionment. The reality of life in post-war Germany was that living standards had plunged and could not be quickly restored. The Ebert Government deserves some credit for managing the demobilisation process, for maintaining essential services and preserving the cohesion of the Reich. But in face of huge economic dislocation, continuing Allied blockade and, following Versailles, the demands from the Allies for deliveries of coal and other raw materials, there could hardly be a swift return to normal. This was the background to the on-going confrontation between the Government and the radical left, of which the Spartacist rising in Berlin had been an early example. There were mass strikes in the great industrial centres of West and Central Germany. It was a great social protest by the workers and the various groups within the hard left were only imperfectly in control of these movements, but did their best to politicise them. They claimed that the elections to the Constituent Assembly were a sham, that Ebert, Noske and Scheidemann were traitors to the revolution, and their slogan was 'all power to the councils', which Lenin had proclaimed successfully in Russia. The strikers recruited their own red militias which engaged in bloody fighting with the Freikorps and Reichswehr troops sent to crush what had developed into armed risings. In March 1919 there were some 1200 dead in Berlin. Noske was always more concerned to maintain the morale of his scratched-together troops than to use minimum force. During the Berlin disturbances of March he issued a notorious order that anyone found with a weapon in his hands was to be shot on sight. In other major cities, Bremen, Hamburg, Brunswick, Dresden, there were similar clashes, sometimes involving the setting up of short-lived Soviet-type republics.

The left-wing uprising with the most important long-term consequences occurred in Munich. The Bavarian monarchy was the first to fall, but the rule of Eisner, the central figure in the revolution and Bavarian Prime Minister after its success, was short. Elections to the Bavarian Parliament (Landtag) in January 1919 gave his party, the USPD, only three seats out of 180. Even together with the SPD his government was in a minority. He was about to resign when he was assassinated, on 21 February 1919. A period of confusion ensued, which led, in April 1919, to the setting up of a Soviet Republic in Munich. After three weeks Freikorps and Reichswehr troops sent with the support of the Berlin Government entered Munich and crushed the Red Republic with a great deal of bloodshed. These traumatic events, in what was still essentially a conservative, agrarian, Catholic country, soon pushed politics well to the right. Bavaria thus became a haven for forces of the radical right, among them the new Nazi Party.

The Kapp Putsch

The unco-ordinated and essentially doomed efforts of the radical left to carry on the revolution pushed the political centre of gravity well to the right in the whole of Germany. It reinforced the outrage about Versailles and the increasing willingness to accept the 'stab-in-the-back' myth among large elements of the German population. Scarcely eighteen months after the revolution there was now an attempt to overthrow the infant republic from the right. It is known as the Kapp Putsch, after one its leaders, a former leading light of the Fatherland Party. 'Putsch' is the German word for an attempt to overthrow the state by force. The immediate cause of the Kapp Putsch was the impending reduction in the size of the Army, to meet the eventual target of 100,000 men imposed by Versailles. Freikorps troops advanced on Berlin and occupied the government quarter. It now became apparent how misplaced was the confidence that Noske, Ebert and others had put in the generals they had used to protect themselves against the uprisings of the left. One of these generals, Hans von Seeckt, who was to lead the Reichswehr until 1926, when he was asked by Ebert whether he could protect the Government replied: Reichswehr does not shoot on Reichswehr. In other words, the regular army had only a conditional loyalty to the elected government of the republic. It would protect it against the radical left, but when basically nationalist counter-revolutionary forces, such as the Freikorps, attacked it, then it neither could nor would act. For the moment, in spite of the attitude of the generals, the Kapp Putsch failed. There was a general strike and even the civil servants in the central ministries in Berlin, though often in sympathy with the plotters, thought the coup premature and ill-planned.

A Republic Without Republicans

The Republican government, which had had to flee from Berlin for a few days, did not benefit a great deal from the restoration of its authority. The trade unions, as the price of calling off the strike, made far-reaching demands for measures of nationalisation and land reform and for cleansing governmental and administrative bodies of counter-revolutionary elements. Ebert, with great regret, had to sacrifice Noske. Although the trade unions then called off the strike, this was not obeyed in those parts of Germany where the radical left was strong. Having just seen off a challenge from the right the Government was immediately pushed into another confrontation with the left. Particularly in the Ruhr there was again a vicious civil war, with Freikorps and Reichswehr fighting Red Guards, with many casualties.

When in June 1920 the first elections to the Reichstag under the Weimar Constitution took place the erosion of support for the republic, compared with what it had been only seventeen months earlier (see page 37), became only too evident from the results:

Table 5.2. The Reichstag elections, 6 June 1920 (per cent)

USPD	17.9
SPD	21.7
DDP	8.3
DVP	13.9
Z + BVP	17.8
DNVP	15.1

The three Weimar Coalition parties, SPD, DDP and Centre, had seen their support decline from over three-quarters to less than half. The SDP had lost heavily to the USPD and many of these lost voters were eventually to find a home in the KPD, perpetuating the deep split in the German labour movement. It was an exaggeration to say that this had become a republic without republicans, but it was certainly true that the new form of government did not command universal acceptance.

The Great Inflation

Germany's disturbed situation was greatly aggravated up to the end of 1923 by what is still regarded as the classic inflation of modern times. Inflation is a condition in which too much money chases too few goods. Money progressively loses its value and unless the process is stopped the currency of the country concerned becomes useless as a means of exchange. War inevitably causes inflation, for goods are produced, and their producers receive money for producing them, but these goods are not for consumption or investment, but are simply for destruction. Thus, all combatant countries experienced inflation during and after the First World War, but Germany was particularly badly affected. Partly this was due to the fact that since the country was unified in 1871 a fully national system of finance had not been established. The power to tax still rested mainly with the separate Länder. Only a limited amount of tax income, chiefly derived from customs duties, went directly to the national government. The rest of the increasingly necessary revenues had to be obtained by the Reich Government from the Länder governments, so that the Reich was often called a passenger of the Länder. Attempts to remedy this problem before 1914 failed, because the interests entrenched in the Länder, for example the Junkers protected by the Prussian three-tier franchise, resisted a solution. In Germany the war could, therefore, not be financed by raising taxation in the way it was done in Britain. In so far as it was not financed simply by printing money, it was done by getting the population to subscribe to huge war loans. Motivated by patriotism the middle classes in particular put much of their savings into such war loans. The assumption was that these loans would gradually be repaid when Germany won the war, because she would then be able to exact reparations from the defeated enemy.

When Germany lost the war and reparations were imposed on her, any chance of repaying these loans with real, rather than paper money, became remote. Even by 1920 it required, on average, fifteen German marks to buy what one mark would have bought before 1914. Some other European countries were, however, experiencing a similar degree of inflation. There was then a window of opportunity, when it might have been possible to stabilise the position (see Table 5.3, page 54). Erzberger, the much maligned politician, who had shouldered the unpopular task of signing the armistice in November 1918 on behalf of Germany, had as finance minister established the national system of taxation that was missing before 1914. Foreign confidence in the German economy and the German currency began to revive when the republic was seen to defeat the Kapp Putsch. It was hoped that a reparations settlement could be negotiated between Germany and the victorious Allies that the Germans could live with.

The window of opportunity closed again, mainly for three reasons. The coalition governments that were in office after the elections of June 1920 were too weak to agree on a taxation package. Secondly, if such a package had been imposed the effect would have been very deflationary. There would, for a time, have been a slump and rising unemployment. Britain and America experienced just such a slump in 1921. Germany largely avoided the slump, because with the renewed inflation leading to a fall of the external value of the mark, German exports boomed. In Germany industrial production increased by 45 per cent from 1920 to 1921 and another 20 per cent by 1922; in Britain there was no increase in 1920 and a fall of 31 per cent in 1921. In Germany the conditions of relative boom enabled wages to be raised, thus weakening the revolutionary drive among the workers. Without a degree of inflation the fragile republic might well not have survived at this moment. Thirdly, the reparations question removed any incentive there might still have been to tackle the inflation problem. In 1921 reparations amounted to nearly a third of the national expenditure of the Reich Government and in 1922 this proportion rose to nearly 70 per cent, amounts quite impossible to raise by normal taxation. Particularly the nationalist parties argued that if Germany put her financial house in order before a reparations agreement acceptable to her had been negotiated, it would simply make it easier for the Allies to exact their pound of flesh. For these three reasons all attempts to halt the inflation failed.

By 1921 it required on average 25 marks to buy the equivalent of one pre-war mark. By 1922 it required 450 marks. From the summer of 1922 hyper-inflation took off and by the end of the year around 1500 marks were needed to equal the purchasing power of a pre-war mark (see Table 5.3, page 54). Any favourable effect the inflation might have had keeping up the level of production and employment vanished in chaos. The trade unions and the SPD became aware that a rise in money wages no longer meant a rise in real wages and that only a levy on the owners of real property could end the vicious spiral of wages and costs. By the same token the owners of real property, mostly the wealthier classes owning houses, factories and similar assets, were unwilling to pay such a levy.

The Beginnings of National Socialism

The political party which became known as NSDAP (National Socialist German Workers Party) had its origins in Bavaria. As we have seen, this essentially conservative, agrarian and Roman Catholic part of the country had been the scene of the short-lived Soviet Republics in the spring of 1919. After this episode Bavarian politics moved well to the right. This Bavarian government was continually at odds with the government in Berlin, partly because the sense of Bavarian independence was still strong, but even more so because the Berlin governments were regarded in Munich as dangerously 'red'. Laws against right-wing subversion, promulgated by the Reich, were disregarded or scarcely applied in Bavaria, which therefore became a refuge for extremist anti-republican elements. A multitude of racialist groups flourished in Munich, 'racialist' being an inadequate translation of the German *Völkisch.* It meant belief in Germans, wherever they lived, as a race, biologically different and superior to other races, therefore an extreme form of nationalism. One of these Völkisch groups, soon making waves through its exceptional violence and extremism, were the National Socialists.

Some of the ideas which motivated many in the Völkisch movement, but particularly the National Socialists, had already been around before 1914. These included the notion that race was the most important factor in history and could be scientifically defined. The discoveries of Darwin about the origin of species through the survival of the fittest were transferred to the sphere of human society, an idea usually called 'social Darwinism'. History was therefore a perpetual struggle between races for supremacy. A race was made and kept superior only through struggle and war. The ultimate law governing human existence had no connection with any morality of right or wrong, but simply consisted of the right of the stronger to prevail. This right applied not only between races, but also within a nation. National Socialism was therefore violently opposed to democracy, parliamentary government, liberalism, all based on the idea that there were some basic human rights and that different viewpoints had a right to exist. National Socialists rejected totally the notion of equality and therefore saw in socialism, usually based on the intellectual schemes of Karl Marx and his predictions of revolution, an enemy to be eradicated. Anti-Semitism was to be found in all Völkisch groups, nowhere in more extreme form than in National Socialism. The Jews were seen as a racial, not a religious, group undermining by their presence the cohesion of races like the German. They were also held responsible for the ideologies that upheld the equality of all human beings, from Christianity to socialism, and particularly the latest threatening form of socialism, the Bolshevism that had just triumphed in Russia. At the same time they were blamed for international capitalism and out of this was constructed a theory of a Jewish world conspiracy. The Jews were seen as the promoters of all the modern tendencies which attracted the hatred of those drawn to the Völkisch movement.

Fascism and Nazism

- The period after the First World War favoured the rise of movements which came to be called 'Fascist' not only in Germany, but all over Europe.
- The term Fascism came from the Italian movement of this type, led by Mussolini, the first actually to achieve power, in 1922.
- There are some features which are characteristic of all the parties of the Fascist type, including National Socialism, which in due course was to become the most important and the most radical of all these movements.
- Common to Fascism was faith in strong government built round a leader (in Italian 'Duce', in German 'Führer'). This was the way the masses, now fully participant in politics, having as soldiers had to risk their lives in the war, were to be controlled and turned away from the parties of the left, from socialism, Marxism and revolution.
- Although Fascism was located at the opposite end of the political spectrum from socialism or communism, it borrowed both ideas and tactics from its opponents. Fascism appealed to social groups who wanted to conserve and stabilise, as they faced the threat of change and modernity, but it was itself revolutionary in its aim to achieve a new and more coherent society.
- Extreme nationalism, the cultivation of military virtues and the use of military formations and of violence in the conduct of politics, were all hallmarks of Fascist movements.
- All Fascist movements have some things in common: authoritarian government, a strong leader (Duce, Führer), paramilitary forces, the use of violence.
- Nazism is the most important and extreme form of fascism, therefore not fully covered by the term 'Fascist'.
- Some Fascist movements in less industrialised societies, Italy, Spain, the Balkans, were less radical, less revolutionary and more conservative than Nazism.

Documents. From Hitler's *Mein Kampf* (Chapter 14), on foreign policy
... the foreign policy of the Völkisch state must safeguard the existence on this planet of the race embodied in the state, by creating a healthy, viable natural relation between the nation's population and growth on the one hand and the quantity and quality of its soil on the other hand ... the National Socialist movement must strive to eliminate the disproportion between our population and our area - viewing this latter as a source of food as well as a basis for power politics ... the demand for the restoration of the frontiers of 1914 is a political absurdity ... for in reality they were neither complete in the sense of embracing the people of German nationality, nor sensible with regard to geo-military expediency ... if we speak of soil in Europe today, we can primarily have in mind only Russia and her vassal border states in Russian Bolshevism we must see the attempt undertaken by the Jews in the twentieth century to achieve world domination ...

From Hitler's *Mein Kampf*, on propaganda
The receptivity of the great masses is very limited, their intelligence is small, but their power of forgetting is enormous. In consequence of these facts, all effective propaganda must be limited to a very few points and must harp on these slogans until the last member of the public understands what you want him to understand by your slogans

From Hitler's *Table Talk*, 11 July 1941
... the greatest blow that ever struck humanity was the coming of Christianity. Bolshevism is Christianity's illegitimate child. Both are inventions of the Jew. The deliberate lie in the matter of religion was introduced into the world by Christianity. Bolshevism practises a lie of the same nature, when it claims to bring liberty to men, whereas in reality it seeks only to enslave them ...

- The Nazi ideology is very imprecise, it is what the Führer at any given moment says it is, and is therefore very flexible in its tactics.
- In its early days Nazism was anti-capitalist, because it appealed to lower-middle class groups squeezed between big business and unionised labour. After 1929 the Nazis were less anti-capitalist, because they wanted support from the middle classes and big business.

The Personality and Ideas of Adolf Hitler

The general notion of Fascism can be used only within limits to explain the German variety, National Socialism. Not only was Nazism, the shortened, popularly current version of the name, more radical and more important, it was also less fixed and more fluid. This is largely due to the fact that Nazism consisted predominantly of the ideas and the actions of one man, Adolf Hitler, so that it has often been simply called Hitlerism. Hitler was born in 1889, on the German-Austrian border, the son of a minor Austrian customs official. His background is shrouded in obscurity and he was always anxious to keep it so. When his troops took over Austria in 1938 he made sure that all evidence concerning his early life was removed and one or two of his early associates were murdered on his orders. The account of his early life which he gives in his book *Mein Kampf* (My Struggle) is totally unreliable. There is even a possibility, which cannot now be proved or disproved, that one of his grandparents was Jewish. We do know that he led a hand-to-mouth existence in Vienna from about 1907 to 1912. There was great tension between how he wanted to see himself, as a great artist or other great man, and the reality of his existence. During this time he acquired many of the ideas to which he clung all his life, the superiority of the Aryan (Germanic) race against the inferior Slav races then making up the Habsburg empire of which Vienna was the capital and the virulent hatred of the Jews as the originators of all the things Hitler despised. He also gained insights into what motivated those at the bottom of the heap in a large modern city. He had nothing but cynical contempt for the masses. Later he wrote in *Mein Kampf* that they were incapable of absorbing anything complicated and could be manipulated only through the repetition of a few simple ideas, even if they were lies. The bigger the lie the better.

When faced with service in the Austrian Army, which as part of the multi-racial Habsburg empire he held in contempt, he moved to Munich. At the outbreak of war in 1914 he enlisted in the Bavarian Army, in which he fought with bravery. He won both the second and the first class of the Iron Cross, rare for a non-commissioned officer. Like so many others, Hitler's personality was deeply influenced by the war. It was the only time in his life when he had any kind of ordered existence or recognised job. It reinforced the 'social-Darwinistic' outlook which was at the core of his mental world. Twenty years later, when he had become the dominant force in world politics, he was the one major leader who believed that war was in the nature of things, whereas almost everybody else feared it deeply or thought it justified only as an ultimate recourse.

Hitler Becomes a Politician

When Hitler returned to Munich after the war he was reluctant to return to civilian life, in which he had never been able to make out. For a time the Army used him as a political informer, to spy on the many meetings that were going on in a city racked by revolutionary disturbances. It was thus that the possibility of engaging in political activity as a form of employment became apparent to him. He joined one of the small groups in the Völkisch movement, which called itself German Workers' Party and met in the back-room of a beer cellar. It became clear that he had an exceptional gift for speaking to audiences of this kind. He could sense what grievances were nagging his listeners and then, like a medium, express their fears and frustrations. He could use extreme verbal violence with great effect, attacking the republican politicians, whom he always called 'the November criminals', the Jews, the Marxists and whoever else came into his sights. Through Hitler's ability as an agitator larger audiences were attracted and bigger halls could be hired. The party was refounded as National Socialist German Workers' Party and a twenty-five point programme adopted at what was regarded as the foundation meeting, on 24 February 1920. The programme contained many of the planks that were at this point the normal fare of Fascist and Völkisch groups. There was the extreme nationalism, underpinned by a racial view of what German meant, mentioning particularly the exclusion of Jews. There was also a good deal of anti-capitalism, giving substance to the inclusion of 'socialism' in the party's title. The anti-capitalism included cranky ideas, for example that the levying of interest payments was a form of usury and should become illegal. Hitler declared this programme immutable, but it was never of great importance in the rise of Nazism. In due course the ideology was what Hitler declared it to be, therefore infinitely flexible and adaptable to the tactical requirements of the moment. The anti-capitalism was important in the early days of the movement, when it was recruiting itself largely from the lower middle class. It was less useful when the NSDAP was becoming a mass movement after 1929 and strove to make itself look respectable. From this point of view even the anti-Semitism could be counterproductive and was slightly pushed into the background, though never absent, in the period between 1929 and 1933. Nevertheless, the general orientation implicit in the programme, if not the details, remained characteristic of Nazism.

The Use of Violence

Hitler soon made himself undisputed master of the Nazi Party and became a force to be reckoned with in Munich politics. He collected around himself a clique, some of whom reached high positions in the Third Reich. Already he had an unusual, monstrous will and ability to dominate. It is therefore not too far-fetched to give National Socialism the label Hitlerism. These post-war years were, as we have seen, a period of violence in German politics and Hitler was well aware of the uses of violence for his movement. It could instil fear in opponents, command attention and form an attraction for certain types of followers. The NSDAP established from small beginnings its own paramilitary force, the stormtroopers, the SA (*Sturmabteilung*). It was used to protect its own meetings, break up those of its opponents and create an atmosphere of violence and terror on the streets. The Bavarian Government and the police authorities in Munich were up to a point willing to tolerate this violence from the right as a counterweight to a possible renewed revolutionary upsurge from the left. Recruitment to the SA was facilitated by the insistence of the Allies on a dissolution of the Freikorps, as part of German disarmament, and many

Freikorps fighters found refuge in the SA. By 1923 Hitler had at his disposal a considerable paramilitary force, perhaps thirty thousand strong, though still only one, if the most violent, of the many paramilitary formations flourishing in Bavaria and elsewhere in Germany. Hitler was not able to solve satisfactorily the relationship between the SA and the Nazi Party. He saw the SA as one arm of his ultimately political battle, but the stormtroopers regarded themselves as the core of the party and a law unto themselves. The tail was liable to wag the dog and at the time of the Beer Hall Putsch Hitler was virtually forced into action by his impatient stormtroopers. The use of symbols to inspire the loyalty of the faithful and frighten opponents was part and parcel of all Fascist movements. Hitler personally concerned himself with working out the details of the Nazi symbols. The SA wore brown shirts, the swastika, a symbol frequently on show among Völkisch groups, was adopted in the form that was eventually to inspire fear and loathing all over the world.

The Crisis of 1923

In 1923 the state of Germany became critical and for nearly a year not only the survival of the republican constitution but the continued existence of a unified Reich hung in the balance. The crisis began with the occupation by French and Belgian troops of the Ruhr in January 1923. This was Germany's most heavily industrialised area, containing much of her coal, iron and steel industries. It lay east of the River Rhine, with major cities like Düsseldorf, Essen, the home of the firm Krupp, and Dortmund. It had not hitherto formed part of the zone west of the Rhine occupied by Allied troops, including the British, under the terms of the Treaty of Versailles. The underlying reason for the French move was that the Versailles settlement had left them feeling insecure. In return for their failure to back the French desire for a division of Germany at Versailles, Britain and the United States promised a watertight treaty of assistance in case of a renewal of German aggression. Such a treaty was never concluded. Reparations gave the French a lever to engage in German affairs and the German inflation was regarded in Paris as an attempt to evade them. In 1922 Germany concluded the Treaty of Rapallo with Russia. Its terms were not far-reaching in themselves, but the treaty further fuelled French suspicions. Rapallo became a byword for German preparedness to turn to Russia, even under the Bolshevik regime, for support against the West. The two outcast nations of Europe might get together to undo the Versailles settlement. The French justified their march into the Ruhr by claiming that the Germans had failed to deliver previously agreed coal and wood reparations consignments. In the longer run the French hoped to achieve what they had failed to obtain at Versailles, an autonomous Rhine-Ruhr region linked at least as much to France as to Germany. Raymond

Poincaré, at this moment the French Prime Minister, was the principal mover behind this policy.

The French move caused an outcry in Germany, comparable in its intensity to the nationalist emotions aroused by the outbreak of war in 1914. The Germans lacked the means to resist France militarily, but the German Government backed a campaign of passive resistance. All German officials were ordered to refuse any collaboration with the occupying forces and this was also the attitude of the vast majority of the Ruhr population. The French found it initially very difficult to get any coal, steel and other materials out of the Ruhr, because employers and workers refused to produce them or allow them to be transported. There was an increasing number of violent incidents and acts of sabotage, to which the occupiers responded by executions and imprisonment. Gradually the German ability to offer passive resistance declined and by September 1923 the German Government was forced to call off the campaign. In the meantime the Reich had had to spend vast sums to pay the salaries and wages of the Ruhr population, while increasingly losing any access to the area's productive resources. As a result the German currency lost all its value. A kilo of potatoes cost 92,000 marks on 3 September, three weeks later it cost 1.24 million marks. The average price of the dollar in Berlin was 110,000 marks in June 1923; in September it was nearly 100 million marks and in October it was over 25 billion marks. As the value of the mark plunged hourly, any adjustment of wages to prices became meaningless. Washing baskets full of banknotes, used in paying wages, became valueless.

Table 5.3: Dollar quotations for the mark, monthly averages, 1914 and 1919-23

Year	Month	Marks
1914	July	4.20
1919	January	8.90
1919	July	14.00
1920	January	64.80
1920	July	39.50
1921	January	64.90
1921	July	76.70
1922	January	191.80
1922	July	493.20
1923	January	17,972.00
1923	July	353,412.00
1923	August	4,620,455.00
1923	September	98,860,000.00
1923	October	25,260,208,000.00
1923	15 November	4,200,000,000,000.00

The political consequences of this economic and social disaster were devastating. The continued unity of the Reich was seriously in doubt. The

French attempt to separate the Rhine-Ruhr region from Germany, at least economically, looked increasingly likely to succeed. Even before the German Government was compelled officially to call off passive resistance, both employers and workers in the Ruhr were moving towards an accommodation with the occupiers. In Bavaria the right-wing forces, with Hitler and the Nazis in the van, were moving towards a coup, followed by a march on Berlin. They were spurred on by the example of Mussolini, who a year earlier had seized power in Italy by marching on Rome. The right-wing revolt in Bavaria was given impetus by the possibility of a left-wing take-over in Saxony and Thuringia, on Bavaria's northern border. Here Communists had joined Social Democrats in coalition governments and so-called 'Proletarian Hundreds' were being armed in preparation for an uprising. In Moscow it was hoped that the German 'October', the long delayed red revolution, would now actually occur.

Hitler's Beer Hall Putsch

In Bavaria Hitler's beer hall putsch was crushed on 9 November 1923. He had used the occasion of a political meeting in one of Munich's beer cellars, at which the principal personalities of the Bavarian Government were present, to force them into the march on Berlin. He knew that the Bavarian leaders, so long tolerant of his violent movement, were now hoping that the democratic republican government would be overthrown and an authoritarian right-wing government put in its place to clear up the mess. The Bavarian leaders saw themselves as a vital bastion of support for such a coup. They were, however, not prepared to allow their hand to be forced by Hitler. They had never seen him and his rough-neck stormtroopers as

Inflation currency: from 1 mark (1914 note) to 100 million (24 September 1923)

more than useful footsoldiers in their efforts to defeat the left. Threatened by Hitler with force, they pretended to go along with him while in the beer cellar, but as soon as they had regained their freedom of movement they assembled loyal troops and crushed his uprising. Sixteen Nazis were killed and later, in the Third Reich, celebrated as martyrs of the Nazi movement. Hitler was imprisoned and put on trial. From this failure he learnt the lesson that an overthrow of the government against the forces of law and order is virtually impossible in a modern state. The road to power lay through the ballot box and through a pretence of legality.

End of the Crisis

In the meantime, the chances of a successful left-wing revolution in Central Germany had also been scuppered. The Reich Government, which had shown itself impotent in dealing with the defiant authorities in Munich, adopted a much firmer line against the left-wing governments in Saxony and Thuringia. The 'Proletarian Hundreds' were dissolved by the Army and the Communists were forced out of government. An unco-ordinated Communist rising in Hamburg was crushed. Never again was there any realistic chance of a revolution from the left, though the fear of it continued to affect political attitudes and strengthened the right.

Finally the inflation, the prime cause of the political radicalisation, was ended. It had become clear that a new currency had to be introduced and its issue so tightly controlled that it would become a means of exchange in which people could have confidence. On 20 November 1923 this new currency, called the *Rentenmark*, was brought in. A thousand billion marks were exchanged for one mark. The operation was a success, but of all the disasters that had afflicted Germany since 1914 none left deeper resentments.

- Before 1914 money had been remarkably stable in value all over Europe, including Germany.
- People therefore found it hard to imagine that money could lose its value and many kept their savings in banks and similar deposits.
- It is for this reason that they subscribed without qualms to the war loans issued by the government during the war.
- They were entirely unprepared for the loss of their savings through inflation, did not adapt in time and were left penniless.
- Others who had assets such as houses or were smart enough to acquire them, often for not more than a song during the inflation, were sitting pretty.
- Those gullible enough to part with such assets, or forced to do so to make ends meet, were losers.
- The wealthy and the owners of the larger businesses, accustomed to dealing with financial affairs, did well. Middle-class people who had

saved up for their old age or to give their children a good education were hard hit.

- The injustice of it all made many people permanently disaffected towards the republican regime, even when it entered calmer and more prosperous waters.

The Government and Inflation

- Germany financed the First World War by borrowing, not from taxation. After victory she would recoup herself from her defeated enemies.
- Weimar governments were too weak and divided to end the inflationary spiral.
- For a time Germany benefited from the weakness of her currency and did not experience the severe slump other nations, including Britain and the USA, did in 1921.
- Reparations were an additional reason why Germany was not motivated to put her finances in order.
- The French occupation of the Ruhr and German passive resistance to it knocked the bottom out of the German currency.

Stresemann, Weimar's Strong Man

During the critical three months, from August to November 1923, a coalition government was in power in Germany, which stretched from the SPD on the left to the DVP, the right-wing liberal party, on the right. Its head was Gustav Stresemann, who emerged as the strong man of the republic (see page 15). He wanted to recover her place as a Great Power, but saw that this could only be done by patient negotiations with her former enemies and by regaining their trust. Above all, he knew that Germany's underlying economic importance would be the most crucial factor in her rehabilitation. In Britain and America it was realised that the world economy could not recover from the consequences of the war unless there was also an economic recovery in Germany, one of the three major industrial economies of the period. There was increasing impatience in the Anglo-Saxon countries with the French policy, under Poincaré's leadership, of imposing a kind of aggravated version of Versailles on Germany. Stresemann hoped to use these differences in the Allied camp to Germany's advantage, but he was realistic enough to know that he could not count on a real split in the long-standing Anglo-French entente. Within a few weeks of becoming Chancellor, Stresemann had ended the policy of passive resistance in the Ruhr, because it was clearly no longer capable of being maintained. For this the nationalist right in Germany vilified him as a traitor. His days as Chancellor were numbered when the SPD left his government, because he was unable and unwilling to treat the rebels of the extreme right in Bavaria with the same severity he meted out to the revolutionaries of the extreme left in Saxony. The new currency was introduced just before Stresemann's fall as chancellor, but he was retained as foreign minister in all the many coalitions formed until his death in October 1929. He therefore can be regarded as the chief architect of Germany's recovery after 1923.

Stabilisation and Recovery

The ending of hyper-inflation and the introduction of a stable currency were essential for Germany's recovery, but this recovery could have made no progress without international agreements, implying Germany's rehabilitation within the family of Western nations. The first necessity was a settlement of the reparations problem, for without this the mark would again be undermined. Such a settlement would, however, also require a big shift in the French position, because reparations could then no longer be used as a lever against Germany and the French occupation of the Ruhr would have to come to an end. This was greatly facilitated by the fact that, even in France, Poincaré's policy of coercing Germany was increasingly seen as a failure. He was replaced as Prime Minister by the more conciliatory Edouard Herriot in May 1924. Even before this had happened a plan had been evolved by a commission under the American banker Charles Dawes to settle the reparations question so that it could no longer damage international relations. Although the United States remained isolationist and unwilling to enter into any political commitment in Europe, it was realised in Washington, and particularly by American businessmen and bankers, that America had a vital interest in the economic well-being of Europe. Regardless of Germany's eventual obligations, the Dawes Plan inititially restricted her payments to one billion marks a year, rising within five years to two and a half billions. The transmission of these sums would be carefully supervised so that the external value of the mark would not be damaged. Credits, mainly from America, would be made available to start the process rolling. The withdrawal of French troops from the Ruhr, beginning immediately and to be completed within a year, was also part of the deal. Although the incorrigible nationalists in Germany regarded the Dawes Plan as tantamount to another Versailles, wiser counsels prevailed. Even a considerable number of the Reichstag deputies of the DNVP, the nationalist party, finally voted for an acceptance of the Dawes Plan in August 1924.

The Locarno Treaties

The economic settlement paved the way for political reconciliation. By early 1925 there were moves towards solving the problem of European security by a pact, which was eventually signed at Locarno in October. The essence of Locarno was that Germany recognised her western boundaries as fixed at Versailles as permanent. This meant acknowledging the loss of Alsace-Lorraine as irreversible. Germany did not offer the same guarantee of her eastern borders, where her territorial losses to Poland had been even greater than in the West. She did, however, undertake never to use force in attempting to change these eastern borders. The Locarno agreements were even more fiercely contested in Germany than the Dawes Plan. The nationalists regarded them as a surrender. Only the votes of the SPD, committed to peace and international understanding, ensured their passage through the Reichstag. In the next few years further progress was made towards bringing Germany back into the ranks of the Western powers. In September 1926 she became a member of the League of Nations. Various provisions of the Treaty of Versailles concerning zones of occupation and supervision of German disarmament were relaxed. The basis of the more peaceful state of Europe in the middle 1920s was Franco-German reconciliation. There was a good relationship between the foreign ministers of the two countries, Stresemann and Aristide Briand. It looked at times as if the degree of European co-operation and unity achieved after the Second World War would come two decades earlier. After 1927 progress began to stall and the highest hopes placed in 'the spirit of Locarno' were disappointed.

In 1926 Germany also concluded another agreement with the Soviet Union, to put Russian fears at rest about Germany ganging up with the West against them. Stresemann never thought that a Russian alliance could be a substitute for Germany's reintegration with the West. He had no time for the ideas, particularly held by Seeckt, the Commander-in-Chief of the Reichswehr until his dismissal in 1926, that Germany should work with Russia, even under a Bolshevik regime, to end once more, if necessary by war, the independence of Poland. Successive governments in Berlin did, however, turn a blind eye to the clandestine collaboration between the Reichswehr and the Red Army in weapons development. It was for Germany a way of evading the restrictions of the Versailles Treaty on their armed forces. There is still a historical debate whether the policies, mainly linked with the name of Stresemann, were simply part of the old nationalist agenda of restoring Germany as a great and eventually again predominant power in Europe. Stresemann himself and his supporters had to defend themselves constantly against vicious nationalist attacks and sometimes claimed more for their achievements in restoring German power than they intended or the facts warranted. Stresemann was enough of a realist to appreciate that the economic interdependence of the major western nations, particularly Germany, had advanced a long way. The kind of power-political drive for exclusive supremacy that he himself had supported during the First World War was no longer sustainable. It cannot be disputed, however, that the relaxations of the Versailles provisions achieved in the days of Weimar formed a favourable jumping-off ground for the brutal aggressions of Hitler. That was not the fault of Stresemann or the other politicians of that era.

Weimar's 'Golden Years'

The political and economic recovery of Germany from 1924 was striking, so that the phrase 'golden years' is often applied to this period. We now know that it did not last and ended disastrously. Hindsight should not blind us either to the reality of the improvement, as it was experienced by contemporaries, nor lead us to suppose that the continuing political and economic problems made the eventual collapse of this first democratic regime in Germany inevitable. The ending of hyper-inflation and the introduction of a stable currency had an immediate calming effect on the political situation and the extremes of left, the Communists, and right, the Nazis and their associates, lost ground. This can be seen from the results of the two Reichstag elections that took place in May and December 1924:

Table 5.4: The Reichstag elections, 4 May and 7 December 1924 (per cent)

	May	Dec.
KPD	12.6	9.0
SPD	20.5	26.0
DDP	5.7	6.3
DVP	9.2	10.1
Z+BVP	16.6	17.2
DNVP	19.5	20.5
NSDAP	6.5	3.0

Nevertheless, it continued to be difficult to provide strong and stable governments and this middle period of Weimar saw a series of shifting and weak coalitions. The SPD remained out of government, hoping thereby to recover some credit with the voters. It continued to be a party of the proletariat, using the language of the class war, necessary to avoid being outflanked by the KPD. This made it difficult for the SPD, the party most closely associated with the republican regime, to collaborate with the so-called bourgeois parties in the maintenance of that regime. The SPD did, however, consistently support the foreign policy of conciliation pursued by Stresemann. At the other end of the political spectrum the DNVP, previously strongly anti-republican, became sufficiently reconciled to the parliamentary system to participate in several of the coalitions of the middle 1920s. The landowners and farmers supporting the DNVP knew that unless the party took part in the parliamentary system their interests would be neglected. Nevertheless, there were still many in the party, and in the big veterans organisation associated with it, the *Stahlhelm* (Steel Helmet), who continued to regard the republic as a virtually treasonable system planted on Germany by her enemies. They rejected Versailles, Locarno, the League of Nations, and hankered after a violent, if increasingly unlikely, removal of these uncomfortable realities. They looked back to the imperial era with nostalgia.

The strength of this kind of sentiment can be seen in the election of Hindenburg as President of the Republic, following Ebert's death in February 1925. Hindenburg won the presidency narrowly and, to the regret of nationalist extremists, indicated that he would loyally abide by the republican constitution. Optimists regarded his election as a bonus for the republic, for those lukewarm towards it might now find it easier, with a substitute emperor in place, to accept it. For the time being this may have been so, but when crisis once more struck Germany after 1929 it proved a grave weakness for the democratic system that the man meant to be its highest guardian had so little real commitment to it. In spite of the continuing lack of legitimacy of the Weimar Republic in the eyes of at least a substantial minority, it began to look increasingly permanent. Even the weakness and instability of coalition government is easily exaggerated. Important ministers continued to head the same department from one coalition to another, Stresemann being the most notable example. There was a strong civil service supplying continuity of policies. Many of the Länder governments enjoyed stability, particularly the important Prussian one. Even the Bavarian Government ceased to be indulgent towards the extreme right. It was therefore not so much the case that the German parliamentary democracy was exceptionally weak and unstable, but that so many Germans would still have preferred a more authoritarian system. They did not like the inevitable confusions of a pluralist society and believed that you could somehow have a state that was above politics.

Weimar's Economy

The more settled state of politics in the middle years of Weimar rested on greater economic stability and prosperity. By 1928 the German standard of living was slightly better than it had been in 1913. Germany had not quite recovered her pre-war standing as an international trading nation, but neither had Britain. The United States had emerged as the great beneficiary of the economic upheaval caused by the war. From 1924 the German economy had become very dependent on the in-flow of American capital and this became damaging when, after the Wall Street crash of October 1929, the American economy went into a deep slump. For the time being, American and other foreign investors were happy to put their money to work in Germany, which seemed to be enjoying a striking recovery from the ravages of war and inflation. It now became possible to satisfy some of the expectations aroused among the masses by the revolution of 1918. In 1927 a comprehensive system of unemployment insurance was established, under which employers and employees each contributed 3 per cent of wages to an insurance fund. It was the completion of the German welfare system begun by Bismarck in the 1880s.

Weaknesses of Weimar in the mid-1920s

- Prosperity depended on the influx of foreign capital, which was withdrawn after the crash of 1929.
- The market did not operate freely in either capital or labour: there were many monopolistic cartels and wages were fixed by binding arbitration.
- The national opposition was still not reconciled to the republic and at the other end of the political spectrum the support of the liberal intelligentsia was also lukewarm.
- Historians analysing the German economy during this more prosperous period have emphasised the shortcomings which, to some extent, explain the depth of the slump subsequently experienced.
- Even at the time employers and businessmen complained of the high social costs with which they had been burdened, under the influence, as they saw it, of a strong trade union movement linked to the influential SPD.
- Industry had itself invested rather recklessly during the inflation and now found itself saddled with capacity it could not profitably use.
- To escape the consequences some near-monopolies were created, for example the great chemical combine I.G. Farben, later notorious for its role in the Third Reich.
- On the other side of the economic divide a system of compulsory wage arbitration often worked in favour of the wage earners, but restricted the operation of the labour market.
- Both contemporary and subsequent economic analysts diagnosed a weakening of the market mechanism all round, reducing German international competitiveness. Just as the diverse criticism of Weimar's political arrangements do not justify the assumption that their eventual failure was inevitable, so these economic weaknesses do not mean that the economy was sooner or later heading for collapse.
- Economic strengths and weaknesses are a matter of swings and roundabouts and no economic system works perfectly.
- It is worth reflecting that the level of consumption which the ordinary German enjoyed in 1928 was hardly reached again in the Third Reich, for Hitler's so-called economic miracle in the 1930s was mainly based on preparation for war and brought little benefit to the consumer (see Table 9, page 115).

Weimar's Culture

Weimar had a vigorous cultural life. Writers like Thomas Mann and Bertolt Brecht wrote books and plays which are still read and performed all over the world even today. In many other fields, music, architecture, the new medium of film, Weimar Germany was home to developments that remain influential to the present day. Berlin was a vibrant metropolis, to which people from all over the world came for a taste of what was new and modern. Weimar Germany was exceptionally exposed to the fascinations and pitfalls of modernity, for so many of the gods that had ruled German society in the past had been dethroned by defeat and revolution. It is now clear that some of the intellectual and artistic trends associated with the Weimar period were already in evidence before 1914, but the collapse of traditional values gave them a freer rein after 1918. By the same token, many of those who looked back to the days of imperial glory with nostalgia, those on the conservative and nationalist side, looked upon Weimar modernity, Berlin and all that went with it, with disgust and hatred. At least as widely read as the still famous books of the left-wing and liberal writers were books glorifying war and the heroism of the German nation. Nationalist and right-wing hatred of Weimar's free-thinking intelligentsia was often tinged with anti-Semitism. Many of the well-known writers, artists and journalists were Jewish. About a third of German Jews lived in Berlin, although overall they formed less than 1 per cent of the population. Weimar's liberal intelligentsia was itself often less than wholehearted in defence of the republic which protected their freedom. Those on the Communist left naturally attacked Weimar as bourgeois and wanted it replaced by a socialist regime. Even the less doctrinaire liberals were put off by the greyness and lack of charisma of Weimar politicians and by the many inevitable flaws in the political and social system.

Questions to Consider

- What were the weaknesses of the Weimar constitution?
- Was the Treaty of Versailles the greatest reason for the weakness of the Weimar Republic?
- Which was the greater threat to the Weimar Republic: the right or the left?
- Why was the NSDAP founded in Bavaria and how did Hitler become its undisputed leader?
- What was the importance of the 'great inflation' of 1923 for Weimar politics?
- What were the characteristics of Germany during Weimar's 'golden years'?

EXAMINATION QUESTIONS

1. 'A fairly lenient treaty.' Is this a just comment on the Versailles Treaty?
2. Was the Weimar Republic doomed from the outset?
3. 'In view of its difficulties, the Weimar Republic was very successful.' Do you agree?
4. Why did the Weimar Republic survive longer than the Third Reich?

6 The Destruction of Democracy

Weimar Politics on the Eve of the Great Depression

It is beyond dispute that there was much about Weimar democracy that was unsatisfactory and fragile. Above all, it was not a system that commanded the general acceptance of the population. Parliamentary democracy was itself a matter of controversy, accepted perhaps for the time being by a majority, but rejected, with varying degrees of violence, by what was for the moment a minority that could become a majority in adverse circumstances. Nevertheless, few would have foretold in 1928 that within less than five years Germany would be in the grip of the most brutal and radical dictatorship of modern times in the Western world. On 20 May 1928 the fourth Reichstag of the Weimar Republic was elected. The result showed the SPD, the party most closely associated with the Republic, returned as much the largest party, recovering much of the strength it had lost since 1919.

Table 6.1: Reichstag elections, May 1928 (per cent)

Party	Per cent
KPD	10.6
SPD	29.8
DDP	4.9
DVP	8.7
Z+BVP	15.2
DNVP	14.2
NSDAP	2.6
Others	13.9

The Nazis were reduced to a marginal position. Even the major nationalist party, the DNVP, had lost heavily. In the light of what later happened, historians have, however, found features in these results that help to explain the later Nazi electoral breakthrough. The number of voters drawn to small parties listed in the column 'others' had almost doubled since the previous election in 1924, when it had been 7.5 per cent. The position of the two liberal parties, the DDP and the DVP, weakened further, after the slight recovery in December 1924. All this, in addition to the losses of the DNVP, amounted to a fragmentation in the centre of German politics, from which the Nazis were ultimately the main beneficiaries. Alienated middle-class voters had lost confidence in their traditional leaders and were looking for a party to assert their rights forcefully, but had not yet found it. As for Hitler's party, its overall performance was poor. A drive to make converts among the workers in large cities had clearly failed. But in a few farming areas in north-west Germany the Nazis were forging ahead. Small farmers in regions like Schleswig-Holstein and Lower Saxony, where there were some poor farming lands, were under severe financial pressure even in 1927. There had been an international fall in the price of agricultural commodities, heavily mortgaged small farms were driven into bankruptcy and there was some local violence in such areas. The Nazis made a sudden appearance as a major force in some such localities. For the moment it was a purely local phenomenon, but it foreshadowed their later breakthrough. Another group among whom the Nazis made early converts were university students. Many of them came from middle-class homes, whose economic status had been reduced by war and inflation, and their own job prospects were often poor. To these economic pressures were added a fierce nationalism, a revolt against rationalism and a strong aversion from democracy and egalitarianism. Therefore the Nazi ideology became attractive to many students.

The Rebuilding of the Nazi Party

In the middle 1920s the Nazi Party had been rebuilt after the fiasco of the Beer Hall Putsch. Hitler had used his trial in 1924 as a platform to project himself as the leader of a future national rebirth. The Bavarian judges treated him with leniency and his sentence of five years' 'honourable confinement' was commuted by December 1924. The verdict was typical of the nationalist, right-wing bias of many German judges in the Weimar period. While in prison Hitler kept himself aloof from the dissensions and recriminations in the Völkisch movement and also wrote the first part of a self-justifying book *Mein Kampf* (My Struggle) (see documents, page 50). It became the bible of the Nazi movement and was distributed in millions of copies in the Third Reich. *Mein Kampf* and a so-called Second Book, written in 1928 but kept secret, contains all the ideological baggage, anti-liberal, anti-democratic, anti-Marxist, anti-Semitic, for which Hitler was already known through his speeches. None of it was new or original, but it is pulled together into a racially based social-Darwinist world view. Everything is grossly oversimplified and stated in extreme terms, but it is coherent in itself and has a certain plausibility for receptive simple minds. In these books Hitler also puts forward a programme for German foreign policy, the essence of which is the acquisition, by force, of *Lebensraum* (living space) in Eastern Europe at the expense of the inferior Slav races. Russia was in Hitler's view now ripe for dismemberment, having fallen under the sway of the Jewish-Bolshevik world conspiracy. Germany would also have to subdue France, but she should seek the alliance of Britain and Italy in the wars of conquest that would give her an impregnable position on the European continent. Imperial Germany had, in Hitler's view, made a cardinal mistake in seeking world power beyond Europe and continental predominance at the same time, thus attracting too many enemies. Acquisition of living space in Eastern Europe should come first, then Germany would be an impregnable world power anyway. These prescriptions were not remarkably original at the time, the Treaty of Brest-Litovsk during Germany's brief supremacy in Eastern Europe in 1918 having come close to realising rather similar aims. Hitler himself, when he was master of Germany in the 1930s, came again so close to carrying out this programme that *Mein Kampf* has sometimes been seen as a blueprint for his actions. It would be more accurate to see the book as an indication of his general orientation and mind-set rather than as a blueprint. Hitler, no more than anyone else, could foresee the circumstances in which he would have to act and he could be very opportunistic. An attentive reader of *Mein Kampf* would, however, be left in no doubt about the extremism and brutality of Hitler's aims.

In February 1925 Hitler refounded the NSDAP, now entirely independent of all other groups in the Völkisch movement and built totally round himself as the leader. The *Führerprinzip* (leadership principle), that the Führer has the supreme authority in all matters doctrinal and practical, was to become of great importance in the Third Reich. For the moment it enabled Hitler to overcome the tendency to split over aims and tactics, characteristic of all extremist political groups, and to make his party the chief organisation of the Völkisch movement, sometimes called the radical right. Ludendorff, for example, who had previously been regarded as the most important figure on the radical right, was entirely sidelined. Another group, which included the young Joseph Goebbels, later the Nazi propaganda chief, and which emphasised the 'socialism' in National Socialism, was brought under control. Subordinate leaders were sworn, like feudal chiefs, to personal loyalty to the Führer. This was particularly the case with the regional leaders, called *Gauleiter*, of whom there was soon a network throughout Germany. Alongside them there were organisations controlled from the party headquarters in Munich designed to recruit particular groups, such as students, or teachers, lawyers and doctors. These organisations were able later, when Nazism attracted a mass following, to infiltrate and eventually take over many departments of German national life.

The NSDAP became a party well adapted, as it turned out, to the conquest of power, but not nearly so much to the exercise of it, as came to be seen in the Third Reich. It was a chaotic system, held together only by the ultimate authority of the Führer. Hitler himself, at this time as well as later as the dictator of Germany, was averse to all bureaucracy, which did not suit his irregular lifestyle. He left tedious detail to his underlings, provided his own authority was never questioned. It was also a system of 'divide and rule'. For the moment Hitler and his movement were, however, marginalised by the growing stability and prosperity of the Weimar Republic. By 1927 or 1928 most German Länder had lifted the ban, imposed after the Beer Hall Putsch, which prevented Hitler from addressing open meetings. He was no longer seen as a menace and the republican regime was so democratic that it would not censor any viewpoint unless it was a direct threat to public order. Hitler was, in fact, careful to keep within the law, otherwise he would have laid himself open to renewed prosecution. In any case he was now convinced that the way forward was by using all the devices of democrcay, such as elections, while retaining his ultimate aim of doing away with the democratic system. His position as Führer enabled him to impose this line on his followers, even if many of them still hankered after a violent overthrow of the existing order.

The Beginning of Weimar's Final Crisis

After the elections of May 1928 it was almost inevitable that the SPD, as the largest party, should leave opposition and take the lead in forming a government. A Great Coalition was formed reaching from the SPD on the left to the DVP on the right. The latter was Stresemann's party, but it was also the party to which big business, particularly the employers in the Ruhr coal and steel industries, chiefly looked to safeguard their interests. In November 1928 there was a big lock-out of workers in the Ruhr, because the employers claimed that a wage award made by the arbitrator would make them uncompetitive. Although the employers eventually had to beat a partial retreat, the incident showed that important business interests were very dissatisfied with the political system and that they were unlikely to lift a finger to preserve it if it should begin to falter.

By 1929 the German economy was turning sluggish and unemployment was substantially higher than it had been a year before. In May 1929 another incident showed that the parliamentary regime, unlikely to receive much support from the right, was even more directly opposed by the extreme left, the KPD, and that the left was therefore totally divided. The Communists wanted to bring down the 'bourgeois republic', of which the SPD was the main stay. It was the beginning of the phase when the KPD, under direction from Moscow, attacked the SPD as their principal enemy, calling the Social Democrats 'social Fascists'. When the SPD Police Chief of Berlin banned a Communist May Day demonstration, there were violent clashes, with around thirty dead. The KPD claimed that this showed the truth of their contention that the SPD was the real class enemy. One of the major remaining elements of strength of the Republic was in fact the loyalty of most of the police forces, particularly in SPD-controlled Prussia. At least the higher ranks of the police in big cities like Berlin were staunchly republican and prepared to use their forces against attacks on democracy both from right and left.

Referendum on the Young Plan

In the later months of 1929 German politics were overshadowed by the need to negotiate a new reparations agreement to follow the Dawes Plan. This was the Young Plan, named after another American businessman. Germany would have to go on paying reparations until 1988, but the immediate payments were reduced and international supervision, amounting to a curtailment of German sovereignty, was virtually eliminated. The plan was fiercely attacked by the nationalist opposition, who claimed that Germany would remain in servitude for sixty years. The campaign against the Young Plan gave Hitler and the Nazis an early opportunity for national publicity. The main organiser of the campaign was the newly elected leader of the DNVP, Alfred Hugenberg. Under him the party, chastened by its setback in 1928, went over to an all-out attack on the republican regime.

Hugenberg had been a director of the Krupp armaments firm and controlled many newspapers. He also controlled the major German film company, UFA, and film was becoming an increasingly important medium for moulding opinion. He promoted a law, under which any holder of public office, including even the President, Hindenburg, could have been condemned to penal servitude if they signed any agreement or law implementing the Young Plan. The naked extremism of this proposal shows how far the political discourse in Germany had already become debased. Hugenberg was obsessed by the idea that the whole nationalist opposition had to be mobilised against the Young Plan and the republic in general. The violence of the anti-Young Plan proposal was deliberately calculated to bring Hitler and the Nazis to its support. The law was submitted to the referendum procedure allowed under the Weimar Constitution. In December 1929 only 13 per cent of the electorate voted for the proposal supported by Hugenberg and Hitler. Yet the referendum campaign is generally held to have helped Hitler not only to nation-wide publicity but also to have given him raised respectability in the eyes of middle-class voters.

The Great Coalition formed in 1928 remained in office until the Young Plan was voted into law. Most of the parties, other than Hugenberg's followers, the Nazis and the KPD at the opposite extreme, realised that the plan had to be implemented if Germany was to make any progress. Linked to the Young Plan negotiations were efforts to end the remaining Allied military presence in the Rhineland, due to end in any case by 1935. The last Allied troops in fact left on 30 June 1930. It was the final legacy of Stresemann, who died on 3 October 1929, at the age of only 51. After him a less conciliatory tone began to prevail in German foreign policy, particularly in the Franco-German relationship. In the meantime financial and budgetary issues had come to dominate the political scene. The Wall Street Crash of October 1929 foreshadowed a decline in the international economy unprecedented in its severity and duration. This was not immediately obvious and in Germany attention was still focused on domestic economic difficulties. The decline in economic activity and rising unemployment made it increasingly difficult to balance the national budget. The unemployment insurance fund established in 1927 went into deficit and had to be supported from central government sources. Disagreements about how to keep the fund solvent finally led to the collapse of the coalition in March 1930, just after the ratification of the Young Plan. The SPD did not want a greater burden to be put on wage earners, while the industrialists influential in the DVP refused to see higher costs piled on industry. Stresemann was no longer there to restrain his party. There was a feeling in the SPD that a spell in opposition would be better than accepting responsibility for policies resented by the ordinary SPD voter. All attempts to find a compromise between the DVP and the SPD on how to pay for unemployment insurance failed and the Great Coalition broke up. The fall of this last fully parliamentary cabinet was a fateful step in the collapse of the republic.

The End of Parliamentary Government

The fall of the SPD-led coalition had been anticipated by Hindenburg and his advisers, particularly by Schleicher (see pages 16-17), whose period of great influence now began. They were looking towards the installation of a government independent of Reichstag majorities, from which the SPD would be excluded. It would govern by using the President's decree-making powers under article 48 of the Weimar Constitution to enact its legislation. Such a procedure was already used in the days of Ebert to issue the various decrees required by the introduction of a new currency in the winter of 1923/24. But now many saw this step as a way of bringing about a permanent shift in the constitution, lessening the powers of the Reichstag and strengthening those of the President. It meant turning the clock back to something like the constitution of Imperial Germany. As the first chancellor who might govern in this way, without the SPD and with possible resort to article 48, Schleicher had picked Heinrich Brüning (see page 16), the leader of the Catholic Centre Party, the man who was to dominate German politics for the next two years.

He formed a minority government and proposed an austerity budget, designed to balance the Reich budget. When by July 1930 the Reichstag had failed to vote this package into law, Brüning reintroduced it by using Hindenburg's powers under article 48. A majority of the Reichstag could, however, under article 48 declare such presidential decrees invalid, something that had never happened before. A public warning was issued from the President's office that such an adverse vote would lead him to dissolve the Reichstag so that fresh elections would have to follow, something that was stretching the powers given to the president by article 48 almost beyond their limits. The decrees were voted down by 236 to 222 votes and the elections were then fixed for 14 September. It was clear that if they did not produce a result supporting Brüning's policy, then the only option left would be continued government by presidential decree. The only power left to the Reichstag would be once again to vote down whatever decrees the Chancellor would issue. It was equally clear that if the Brüning Government was voted out Germany would be plunged into a crisis that might well end any remaining vestige of democracy and the rule of law. This was exactly what the more extreme opponents of Weimar democracy wanted.

Brüning Rules by Decree

The calling of these premature elections, when the economy was in decline and the Reichstag would have had nearly another two years to run, turned out to be a disastrous miscalculation. Local elections and elections to some of the Länder parliaments had already shown a marked rise of the Nazi vote. It was but a mild foretaste of what was to happen on 14 September 1930:

Table 6.2: The Reichstag elections, September 1930 (per cent)

Party	Per cent
KPD	13.1
SPD	24.5
DDP	3.8
DVP	4.7
Z+BVP	14.8
DNVP	7.0
NSDAP	18.3
Others	13.8

The Nazi vote had increased about eightfold, from around 800,000 to 6.4 million, which, even given the rise in electoral participation from 75 per cent to 82 per cent, was an unparalleled upset. They were now the second-largest party. The SPD was faced with the agonising decision of either supporting Brüning's decrees, hated by most of their followers, or risking the arrival of the Nazis in power. It turned out to be a no-win situation for them and less than three years later this once great party was completely smashed, its leaders and functionaries in concentration camps or exile. As for Brüning, he later claimed, in his American exile, that he had some long-term plan to get through the crisis by bringing to Germany something akin to the British constitution, stable government, headed by a restored monarchy, with the rule of law preserved. At the time there was no sign of such a plan and he was doing little more than hand-to-mouth crisis management. The essence of this was that as the economy continued on its downward spiral, the Brüning Government produced ever more stringent measures to balance the

Document. The Weimar Constitution
Article 48. The Reich President can, if public security and order in the German Reich are substantially disturbed or endangered, take the necessary measures for the restoration of public security and order, if necessary with the aid of armed force ... The Reich President is obliged to inform the Reichstag immediately of all measures taken under paragraphs one or two of this article. If the Reichstag demands it these measures are to revoked.

---

declining revenue with declining expenditure. The Government itself therefore added to the downward, or deflationary pressures, as they are called in the technical language of economists, in the economy. There was now too little money chasing too many goods. The most obvious result of this was ever greater political radicalisation, with Hitler on the right the main beneficiary, but also an increasing Communist vote on the left. In response to this all Brüning could do was to appeal to the people to stand fast until an improvement came.

- The dire consequences of Brüning's failure have led to a major historical debate about possible alternatives to his deflationary policies.
- The alternative would have been the deliberate creation of credit or money, something that came in due course to be associated with the ideas of the British economist John Maynard Keynes.
- Against this it is argued that such Keynesian policies, which in any case ran counter to the prevailing economic ideas, could not in practice be introduced because the German economy was already weak in the 1920s and only the influx of American capital had given an illusion of prosperity. After the Wall Street Crash much of this capital was withdrawn. Only a strict balancing of the national budget could keep Germany afloat.
- There was a strong fear of renewed inflation in Germany, which was shared even in the SPD, which should have been, in theory, in favour of policies reducing unemployment.
- In any case the exceptional severity of the slump was not obvious until the late spring of 1931 and any reflationary measures, as they are usually called, would not have become effective until at least a year or so later.
- These arguments are, in turn, countered by the claim that by the autumn of 1931 the slump was so deep that any deliberate creation of credit, even the simple printing of money, could hardly have been inflationary, as enormous productive capacities were standing idle.
- In fact more and more voices, in industry, the trade unions and even within the government, were advocating just such a policy of credit-creation. Brüning himself thought he could make a virtue of

necessity, by using the increasing misery and political radicalisation to bring about a final end to reparations.

- Reparations were in fact finally abandoned by international agreement in June 1932, but by this time Hindenburg, belying once again his reputation of rock-like loyalty, had dropped Brüning.
- The end of reparations was in any case no longer able to halt the slide into political extremism and near-civil war, because the German voters now had different priorities. They wanted relief from the profound pain and misery of the slump, which would, within eight months of Brüning's fall, bring Hitler to power.

The Fate of the Unemployed

Unemployment was the most obvious result of the slump and the greatest cause of the misery. In the winter of 1932 even official statistics showed something like a third of the German workforce out of work. When the large numbers who simply ceased to look for work are taken into account 40 per cent of those who in normal times might have been in gainful employment were unemployed. Although the Weimar Republic had, as we have seen, built up a remarkably advanced welfare system, it had, after several instalments of the Government's expenditure cuts, virtually ceased to function. As the unemployed ran out of entitlement under the employment insurance scheme, they were temporarily given what was called crisis subvention. When that ran out after a period, they were left to even more meagre local authority hand-outs and often they were left with nothing. Hundreds of thousands of families could not maintain the rent for their dwellings and drifted into shanty towns on the edge of large cities. Others wandered through the countryside, with a few belongings on their back, pushing children in prams, vaguely and vainly looking for work. The suicide rate in Germany in 1932 was 260 per thousand, compared with 133 in the United States and 85 in Britain. The figures for the decline of production during the depression are as striking as those for unemployment. The index for investment goods fell from 100 in 1928 to 35 in 1932, and even the index for the most necessary consumer goods, like food, declined from 100 in 1928 to 85 in 1932. The cost of living declined in the same period from 100 to 80, but there were not many people able to maintain their income on the previous level. In money terms German production had declined by nearly 40 per cent, in real terms by more than a quarter.

The Nazi Party becomes a Mass Movement

The political consequences of this social catastrophe were evident in Länder and local elections throughout 1931 and reached their most devastating level in the many nation-wide ballots that took place in 1932. The votes of unemployed industrial workers went mostly to the KPD. The main effect was that the balance between the two left-wing parties shifted from the SPD, which had about three-quarters of the left-wing vote in 1928, to the KPD, which had about two-fifths by July 1932 and went beyond that in November 1932. This made it easier for the Nazis to raise the bogey of a Communist revolution. In spite of their revolutionary language, the actual ability of the KPD to mount a revolutionary uprising in the early 1930s was almost non-existent. Communist party membership was wildly fluctuating and their capacity to use violence was mostly confined to the poorest quarters of some large cities like Berlin and Hamburg. Here they were engaged in frequent street fights with the Nazis, sometimes for the possession of meeting places in the German equivalent of public houses.

Overwhelmingly the most important political consequence of the economic collapse was, however, the rise of National Socialism into a huge mass movement, roughly twice as large in electoral terms in 1932 as it was already in September 1930. Historians have put a great deal of effort into analysing this upsurge. The Nazis did best among the middle classes in the Protestant parts of Germany. The fragmentation of the middle spectrum of German politics in 1928, the big inroads made into it by the NSDAP in September 1930, led up to a virtual annihilation of the parties other than the Nazis in this spectrum by 1932. In 1928 the two liberal parties and the minor, mostly middle-class parties listed in the column 'others', got 27.5 per cent of the total vote; by July 1932 this had dropped to 4.2 per cent. The nationalist DNVP dropped from 14.2 per cent to 6.2 per cent in July 1932 (see tables 6.1, page 64 and 6.3, page 79). While it would be wrong from these figures to assume that there was a simple migration of the voters from these parties to the Nazis, it is clear that the non-Catholic middle classes now regarded Hitler and his movement as their best hope. The Nazis did less well in Catholic areas, because the two Catholic parties, the Centre and the BVP, on the whole managed to hold on to their voters throughout the crisis. As we have seen, the combined vote of SPD and KPD also held reasonably steady and the Nazis probably did not make too much of an inroad into the industrial working-class areas in the big cities. But many workers in smaller cities and smaller enterprises, who had not in the past voted for the two so-called Marxist parties and had not been members of the main trade unions, did turn to the Nazis. This is also borne out by analysis of the members joining the Nazi Party between September 1930 and January 1933, the period when Hitler moved nearer the threshold of power. About a third of such members, therefore more committed than mere voters, were working class, while workers made up about 45 per cent of the population as a whole. While workers were therefore somewhat under-represented in the NSDAP, they still made up a large part of its support. The Nazis claim that they were not a party, but a movement transcending parties and dedicated to the abolition of the divisive

democratic party system had, therefore, a good deal of truth in it.

Nazism as a Protest Movement

A large part of the population was unfortunately now so disenchanted with democracy that they were quite prepared to abandon it in favour of a strong leader. One can see the huge Nazi vote simply as a protest against the existing state of affairs, rather than as a vote for anything. One Nazi leader, when asked what Nazism really was, replied: 'it is the opposite of everything that now exists'. Contemporaries were often baffled by the Nazi upsurge and attributed it to a lapse of many voters into sheer irrationality,

Election poster, 1932. Our Last Hope. Hitler

driven by despair and whipped up by Nazi propaganda. This seemed borne out by the fact that electoral participation increased from 75.6 per cent in 1928 to 84.15 in July 1932 and that the Nazis seemed to attract a disproportionate number of these previously apathetic electors. There was talk of 'an uprising of stupidity'. Such views were common in the left-wing parties, where the basically rationalist doctrines of Marxism made it particularly difficult to find an effective counter to the appeal of the Hitler movement (see Documents, page 77). It was widely hoped that National Socialism, with its contradictory promises to different groups, would sooner or later fall apart and that the threat would vanish as quickly as it had appeared.

That this did not happen was largely due to Hitler himself and to the operation of the Führerprinzip around which he had rebuilt his movement in the lean years of the middle 1920s. As Nazism became a mass movement with many ramifications and contradictory commitments it was mainly held together by his authority. There was a special tension between the revolutionary aspirations of many rank-and-file Nazis, particularly among the stormtroopers, and the appeal to the middle classes seeking stability and security. In the SA there were many who wanted an immediate seizure

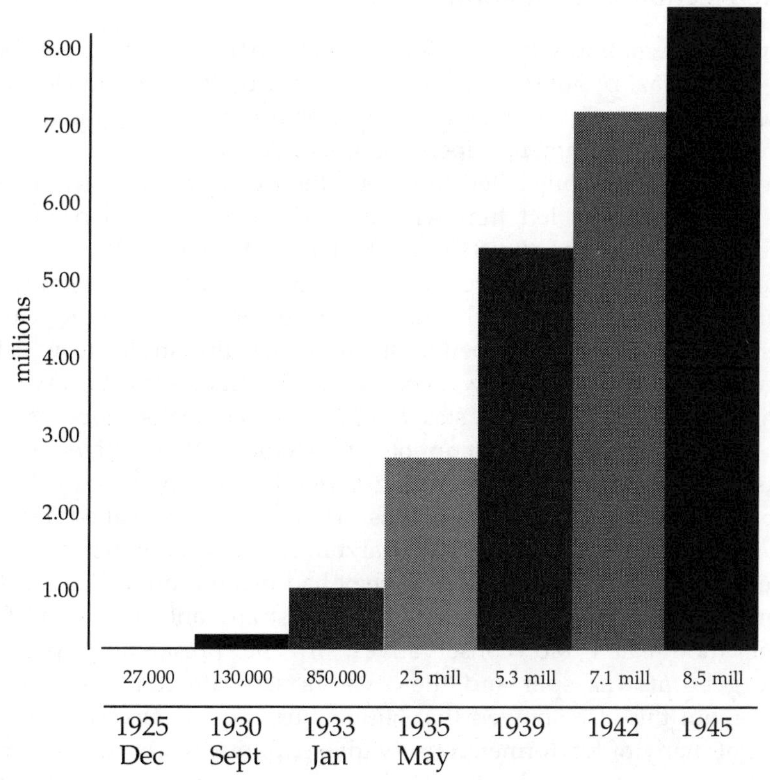

The growth of NSDAP membership. (German population in 1933 was c. 64 million)

of power by force, a bloody reckoning with their enemies and a totally changed society in which they would rule the roost. They were impatient with Hitler's pretence of legality and with the strategy of approaching power through the ballot box. Hitler was faced with several revolts by sections of the SA and the party but managed to ride them out.

The Nazi Vote

- It was predominantly a middle-class vote in Protestant regions.
- Catholics, as well as working-class voters, normally attached to the SPD and KPD, remained the most immune to the Nazi appeal.
- Many workers, from smaller towns and enterprises and not members of trade unions, turned to the Nazis, so that about a third of the Nazi vote was working class.
- Therefore the Nazi claim to be a movement transcending and not a party dividing classes had some truth in it.
- Greater voter participation in the elections after 1928 helped the Nazis.
- There was an element of irrationality and panic, but many felt the 'system' had failed them.

The Re-election of Hindenburg

The first of the nation-wide elections in 1932 that were to reveal the full extent of the Nazi popular support were caused by the need to elect a new president. Hindenburg's seven-year term was due to run out in April 1932. Brüning, whose government depended on Hindenburg, first tried to extend the presidential term, but failed to muster the two-thirds majority required in the Reichstag. This left him with no alternative than to promote the renewed candidature of the 84-year-old Field Marshal. Hitler decided to stand against him and therefore all those who wished to save what was left of parliamentary democracy and the rule of law had to support Hindenburg. Nothing could better illustrate the dire straits to which the Weimar Republic had by now been reduced. Hitler was, however, also running a considerable risk in standing, for the nationalist opposition was by no means united in his support. In October 1931 Hugenberg had organised yet another attempt to bring Hitler's mass movement behind his own by now much smaller battalions. This was the so-called Harzburg Front. A rally had been held at Bad Harzburg, but while Hitler and a large number of stormtroopers attended it, they had made it quite clear that they were now the masters of Germany's nationalist and anti-republican forces, not the moth-eaten old conservatives. In the presidential ballot the Harzburg Front was split and there was a separate candidate from the *Stahlhelm,* but this also showed that Hindenburg no longer commanded the support of many of his former conservative supporters. On the extreme left the KPD put up its own leader, Thälmann. Hindenburg narrowly missed

Documents. 1. Ernst Wilhelm Eschmann, a member of the SPD and trade unionist, about the Communist line in the spring of 1931
Orthodox Communist Marxism has made it easy for itself by turning, with great dexterity, unforeseen movements that pose the greatest danger to the Marxist scheme of things into a confirmation of that scheme. The phenomenon of international Fascism is labelled 'the last throw of capitalism in its attempt to defeat the advancing proletariat'. Thus a phenomenon like National Socialism, which should give rise to the gravest alarm, is turned into a signal of the approaching final victory of the proletariat.
2. Carlo Mierendorff, young socialist intellectual later imprisoned and killed in the Third Reich, on the Nazi success in 1932
There is no denying that apart from all the brutality some very ancient dreams are surfacing. The most potent is that of the 'Third Reich', the mere word envelops the petit bourgeois in nostalgic yearnings ... a ghostly train of perverted memories moves through the semi-proletarian popular memory ... what is serious is not the theory of the National Socialists, but their energy, their fanatical religious quality, which comes not merely from despair and stupidity, but from the strangely stirred up capacity for faith.

getting the required 50 per cent on the first ballot, on 13 March 1932. Four weeks later he was elected with 53 per cent of the vote. Hitler got 30 per cent on the first, nearly 37 per cent in the second ballot, a level that was to prove near the high-water mark of Nazism in any genuinely free election.

The Fall of Brüning

The supporters of the republic derived some reassurance from the results of the presidential ballots. At least for the moment Hitler had been kept out and there seemed to be still enough Germans who wanted at least the rule of law preserved. But its preservation was now in the feeble hands of a very old man nearing senility, who had never been an adherent of parliamentary democracy. Hindenburg resented that Brüning had put him in the position of being elected by the votes of those who were not naturally his supporters, while 'his people', Protestant conservative nationalists, had mostly opposed him. Even more dangerous for Brüning was the fact that Schleicher wanted to be rid of him. As the Nazi numbers mushroomed and the SA grew to several times the size of the Reichswehr, Schleicher and his chief, General Groener, now Minister of Defence in the Brüning Government, became convinced that confrontation with Hitler's movement must be avoided at all costs. Schleicher now wanted a new government, in which the Nazis would be included, but in such a manner that their power was limited. They would thus have to share the responsibility for unpopular measures and they would be 'tamed'. This could not be done with Brüning, who relied on the toleration of the SPD. In fact the one counterbalance to Brüning's dependence on Hindenburg was the continued existence of the SPD coalition with Brüning's own Centre

Party in the government of Prussia. This government tried to put some limit on SA violence, for it still controlled the police forces in two-thirds of Germany. Everybody on the right, from Hugenberg to Hitler, but also the Communists on the left, wanted the end of this SPD-led government. The Prussian Landtag elections of 24 April 1932 came close to bringing this about and again the Nazis got over 36 per cent of the vote, against 1.8 per cent in the previous Prussian Landtag elections in 1928. Along with elections in other German Länder, which also showed big Nazi gains, this was the third major bout of electioneering of the year in crisis-torn Germany.

The days of Brüning were now numbered. The final straw was that the big landowners in the eastern provinces of Prussia attacked him violently for measures to open up heavily indebted estates to settlement by unemployed workers. The landowners called this agrarian Bolshevism and asked Hindenburg to refuse to sign this decree. The President had himself been given an estate in East Prussia in 1927 and was very open to influence by his neighbours. He had always insisted that agriculture in the eastern provinces was given special subsidies, a policy which ran counter to rigid cutting of public expenditure in all other sectors. All this has led historians to conclude that the Junker landowners, although representing a declining economic interest, had, through their access to Hindenburg, greater influence on the events leading to the Nazi dictatorship than did the economically much more important big industrialists. When Hindenburg refused to sign the resettlement decree it effectively meant the dismissal of Brüning. With him went the last republican government enjoying even a vestige of parliamentary legitimacy.

The Death Throes of the Republic

Schleicher had already decided on Brüning's successor. It was Franz von Papen, a virtually unknown politician, who was expected to achieve the elusive 'taming' of Hitler. He constructed a non-party cabinet consisting mainly of aristocratic figures like himself, without even a vestige of popular support. It became known as 'the cabinet of barons'. Part of a potential deal with Hitler was an immediate dissolution of the Reichstag, which had run barely two years of its four-year term. Another part of the deal was the rescinding of the ban on the SA imposed two months earlier. Schleicher was initially in favour of this ban, particularly demanded by the governments in the South German Länder, but then felt that it ran counter to his policy of 'taming' the Nazis. Hitler therefore got a great deal for very little. He got the chance to show the strength of his movement in national parliamentary elections and he secured a free run of the streets for his stormtroopers.

Removal of the Prussian Government

The elections took place in an atmosphere bordering on civil war, with many hundreds killed in street fighting all over Germany. This gave Papen the excuse to remove the SPD-led coalition government in Prussia from office, claiming that it had failed to maintain law and order. This Prussian coup, on 20 July 1932, was another major nail in Weimar's coffin. The control of police forces in Prussia, including Berlin itself, now passed out of hands loyal to the republic. Otto Braun, the Prussian Prime Minister, and Carl Severing, his Minister of the Interior, both from the SPD and known to their opponents as 'the Red Tsars of Prussia', were removed from office. There has been much historical debate about the lack of a strong countermove by the SPD and the free trade unions. It is argued that they should have called a general strike, as they did over the Kapp Putsch twelve years before, and that by giving up without a fight they further demoralised the already weakened support for the republic. It seems unlikely that with a third or more of the work-force unemployed a call for a general strike could have been successful. Ten days later, on 31 July, the Reichstag elections made the Nazis much the strongest party in Germany:

Table 6.3: Reichstag elections, 31 July 1932 (per cent)

KPD	14.5
SPD	21.6
DDP	1.0
DVP	1.2
Z+BVP	16.2
DNVP	6.2
NSDAP	37.4

Germany was now ungovernable, for the two parties dedicated to the overthrow of the parliamentary system, NSDAP and KPD, had a majority. Hitler now demanded to be made Chancellor, with the same ability to make decrees under article 48 as Brüning and Papen had had. He had always kept to the position that, while he would strive for power legally, he would crush his opponents for good, once he had it. He was not prepared to take responsibility and incur rapid unpopularity, without the dictatorial power to make any comeback by his opponents impossible. This, however, Hindenburg was unwilling to grant him. For all his failings and increasing inability to function the old man had a gut feeling that he should not put 'the Bohemian corporal', as he habitually called him, into the chair of Bismarck. This, in fact, kept Hitler out of power for another six months and gives substance to the view that even now his dictatorship, with all its devastating consequences, was not inevitable. On 13 August 1932 Hitler had an interview with Hindenburg, in which the President refused to appoint him Chancellor on the terms he demanded and warned

him against using violence. A communique immediately issued by the President's office turned the occasion into a humiliation for Hitler, the beginning of a series of setbacks.

From Papen to Schleicher

The Papen Government was, however, left with virtually no support in the newly elected Reichstag. It was starkly demonstrated when, at its first meeting on 12 September, it passed a no-confidence motion against Papen by 512 to 41 votes. The Reichstag was immediately dissolved again and fresh elections, the second in 15 weeks and the fifth major bout of national electioneering in 1932, were fixed for 6 November. Nothing was more likely to bring democracy into disrepute. The alternative would have been to risk a formal breach of the constitution and postpone these elections. It was one of the ironies of this protracted crisis that Hindenburg and his advisers clung to the letter of the constitution the spirit of which they had for so long disregarded. Finally, they preferred to hand power to Hitler rather than break the letter of a law which Hitler was dedicated to removing altogether.

That moment had not quite arrived yet and for the time being Papen carried on. He was viciously attacked by both the Nazis and the Communists, between whom there was now a tacit consensus against the democratic republic. In public Papen's cabinet of barons was also vigorously attacked by the SPD, but in private their leaders were aware that worse might follow his downfall. The one major group satisfied with Papen were the industrialists. He removed some of the arrangements, such as wage arbitration, against which business had long argued. He also took some tentative steps towards reflating the economy. In foreign policy he garnered some of the gains, such as the end of reparations, for which Brüning had striven at so very high a cost. The ultimate beneficiary both of reflation and of the progressive dismantling of the Versailles system was to be Hitler. The chief feature of the elections held on 6 November 1932 was a marked decline of the Nazi vote, from over 13 million in July to over 11 million, on a reduced turn-out.

Table 6.4: Reichstag elections, 6 November 1932 (per cent)

KPD	16.9
SPD	20.4
DDP	1.0
DVP	1.9
Z+BVP	15.3
DNVP	8.9
NSDAP	33.1

There were here real signs that the conviction of Hitler's opponents that National Socialism was a flash in the pan and that voters would return to their senses was going to be borne out by events. It looked unlikely that Hitler's balancing act between legality and revolution could be prolonged much further. But the problem how Germany was to be governed was no nearer solution. The various elite groups represented in the Papen Cabinet knew only too well that without mass support no government could survive in the long run and Hitler still had mass support. The last thing the Reichwehr or the industrialists wanted was a return of the SPD to government and they were alarmed by the rise of the Communist vote. Hindenburg was now willing to risk a formal breach of the constitution to sustain Papen, to whom he had taken a great liking. This did not fit in with the ideas of Schleicher. The general did not want to see the Reichswehr having to defend the state against simultaneous attempts at a take-over by Nazis and Communists. Schleicher, inveterate intriguer that he was, hoped that sections of the Nazi movement could be detached from Hitler, and he was also making overtures to the trade union leaders. The government might be sustained by a crossbench alliance, *Querfront* in German.

On 2 December Hindenburg was persuaded to accept Papen's resignation and Schleicher himself took over the chancellorship. Almost immediately a main plank in Schleicher's plans collapsed. He made an offer of the Vice-Chancellorship to Gregor Strasser, at this time regarded by many as second only to Hitler in the Nazi movement and much superior to Hitler, the low-grade demagogue, as a serious politician. He had originally been one of the group who took the socialism in National Socialism seriously and was very much his own man. Unfortunately he had neither the personal following nor the real will to assert himself against Hitler. He was expelled from the party, lived in obscurity, but was still murdered in revenge in the Night of the Long Knives, 30 June 1934. Schleicher fared no better with his trade union contacts, for the suspicion of him in the SPD ran deep. His attempt to present himself as a 'social general' carried no conviction on the left, while it aroused suspicion in the business community, where Papen had been much preferred. Most important of all Schleicher had finally lost the confidence of Hindenburg and attracted the resentment of Papen.

The Final Intrigues

By January 1933 Papen, with the support of Hindenburg, was exploring alternatives to the Schleicher Government, which was unlikely to survive the reconvening of the Reichstag after the Christmas recess. Papen had several meetings with Hitler, at which the possibility was discussed that Papen might after all persuade the President to agree to appoint Hitler Chancellor. Papen would be the real power in such a government, as Vice-Chancellor. Hindenburg remained to the last reluctant to appoint the Bohemian corporal, but a factor that may have helped his entourage, including his son, to persuade him was the danger that the President might

Document. Ludendorff writes to Hindenburg, 1 February 1933

By appointing Hitler Reich Chancellor you have delivered our holy German Fatherland into the hands of one of the greatest demagogues of all times. I solemnly prophesy to you that this accursed man will cast our Reich into the abyss and will bring unfathomable misery to our nation. Coming generations will curse you in your grave for this deed.

---

himself be exposed to scandal. Much of the aid to the big Junker landowners, which had been handed out under pressure from Hindenburg, was thought to have been misappropriated and spent on expensive racehorses and similar luxuries. Hindenburg's own estate, given to him in 1927, had been passed on to his son for the avoidance of death duties. Historians have rightly pointed out that Hitler did not seize power, it was handed to him in a sordid back-stairs intrigue. Ever since the November 1932 elections the Nazi Party had been in deep crisis, losing not only voters, but also members and money. To many it seemed that Hitler's all or nothing gamble had failed and the stormtroopers waiting to settle accounts with their opponents and pick up the loot after a successful coup were deeply disillusioned.

The last piece of the jig-saw puzzle that had to be put in place to enable the Hitler cabinet to be formed concerned the Reichswehr. Schleicher had held the post of Minister of Defence in Papen's and in his own government, but senior generals had become increasingly tired of the way he had dragged the Army into politics. When Hindenburg was assured that an alternative to Schleicher acceptable to the generals had been found, his last qualms about appointing a Hitler cabinet were removed. The post of Minister of Defence was given to General Werner von Blomberg who, unbeknown to Hindenburg, was a Nazi sympathiser and was soon completely taken in by Hitler's personality. The acquiescence of the Reichswehr was vital to Hitler's appointment as Chancellor and to the subsequent consolidation of his dictatorship.

When Hitler and his cabinet were sworn in on Monday, 30 January 1933, only two other ministers, beside the new Chancellor, belonged to the Nazi Party. There was Wilhelm Frick, a man who as an official in the Munich police department had protected Hitler in the early 1920s, and Hermann Göring, who as Minister of Aviation held a portfolio yet to be created, for under the Versailles Treaty Germany had virtually no air force. Göring was, however, also Prussian Minister of the Interior and therefore in control of the police forces in Prussia. He was to use this power ruthlessly in the next few weeks to eliminate opponents of the regime. Hugenberg held the Ministries of Economics and Agriculture and regarded himself as a kind of economic overlord. Even on the left many thought this government was preferable to a Schleicher-Papen government resting on the Reichswehr and therefore amounting to a thinly disguised military dictatorship. Hitler, on the other hand, would come to grief as quickly as his predecessors in the chancellorship. Never was there a greater illusion.

Hitler's Chancellorship

- Hitler's appointment was not inevitable, for the Nazi Party was in decline at that moment.
- There was a fear, without much substance, that the decline of Nazism would benefit the Communists.
- There was a strategy, followed by Schleicher and others, to tame the Nazis by involving them in responsibility.
- The formation of the Hitler Cabinet was an alliance between the Nazi movement and various elite groups, Army, business, landowners, nationalist-conservative sections of the population in general, but it was also the result of intrigues by individuals, Papen, Hugenberg etc.
- There was a failure to appreciate the revolutionary dynamic of the Nazi movement.

Questions to Consider

- What was Hindenburg's part in the destruction of the Weimar Republic?
- Was the economic/financial crisis or political intrigue more important for the achievement of power by the Nazis?
- Which groups did not support the Nazis by 1932?
- 'Too many elections and too many parties.' Is this a fair comment on the Weimar Republic's weakness in 1932?
- 'The failure of the SPD to win more support and to accept power doomed Weimar.' Do you agree?
- Is it fair to claim that Schleicher did more than anyone to bring Hitler to power?

EXAMINATION QUESTIONS

1. Why were the Nazis able to achieve power in the years 1929-33?
2. 'The Weimar Republic was not inherently weak. It collapsed because of ill fortune and poor management.' Discuss.
3. How important was the economic and financial crisis in bringing about the fall of the Weimar Republic?
4. Why, by 1934, had the Nazis benefited more than the Communists from the weaknesses of the Weimar Republic?

7 The Establishment of the Nazi Dictatorship

The 'Taming' of Hitler Fails

If there ever was any coherent plan behind the concept of 'taming' the Nazis it vanished within days, even hours. Hitler immediately pressed for fresh elections, knowing that with the resources of government behind him he was likely to make good the set-back of November 1932 and might even obtain an absolute majority for his party. The elections were fixed for 5 March and in the intervening five weeks the democratic parties met with increasing repression. A decree of 4 February made it possible to suppress their newspapers on the flimsiest pretext. In Prussia Göring recruited stormtroopers as auxiliary police and issued an order that any policeman shooting someone engaged in activities hostile to the state had his full support. Consequently, the republican parties found that their meetings could no longer count on police protection. Some leading republican politicians were beaten up when they addressed their followers. The Nazis were already in almost complete control of radio broadcasting, in the absence of television the most important medium other than newspapers.

The most sensational event of the election campaign was the Reichstag fire on 27 February. It is still not completely clear whether the fire was really started by the lone and demented Dutch Communist van der Lubbe, who was accused of it, or whether the Nazis themselves had a hand in it. What is certain is that it came as a godsend to the Nazis. They could whip up anti-Communist hysteria to fever pitch and on the day following the fire Hitler got Hindenburg to sign a decree suspending the basic liberties of the person, such as freedom from arrest without trial and freedom of speech. This decree of 28 February 1933 remained one of the cornerstones of the Nazi dictatorship until its collapse in 1945. Communist functionaries were arrested in large numbers, including the leader of the party, Thälmann, who was murdered in a concentration camp in 1944. Cleverly Hitler allowed the Communist candidates' names to remain on the ballot papers six days later, even if they were under arrest. The left-wing vote, therefore, remained split. Even so the Nazis failed to obtain an absolute majority, but with their cabinet allies, mainly the DNVP, they had an absolute majority of 52 per cent, 340 out of the 647 seats in the new Reichstag, something no Weimar government had had since March 1930. Hitler had, therefore, achieved his aim of winning power by a show of nominal legality. The turn-out in these last Reichstag elections rose to a remarkable 88.7 per cent and the Nazis obtained over 17 million votes. The result was:

Table 7.1: The Reichstag elections, 5 March 1933 (per cent)

Party	Per cent
KPD	12.3
SPD	18.3
DDP	0.9
DVP	1.1
Z+BVP	13.9
DNVP	8.0
NSDAP	43.9

These elections were a signal for a seizure of power by local Nazis and stormtroopers all over Germany. In villages, towns, right up to the Länder where non-Nazi governments still retained office, public buildings were taken over, the swastika flag was hoisted and Nazi officials were installed. The remaining republican politicians were chased out, often beaten up and paraded through the streets in public humiliation. The SA set up so-called 'wild concentration camps', disused warehouses and similar bunkers, to which opponents of the regime were taken, tortured and sometimes killed. Demoralisation and resignation overtook the republican parties and their leaders and functionaries. In many cases they sought to ingratiate themselves with the new masters by professions of loyalty. All possibility of police protection against or legal redress for the violence committed by the SA had clearly vanished.

A National Uprising

For the bulk of the population, those not actively or prominently associated

Hitler portrayed as a national hero in a line stretching from Frederick the Great

with the previous republican regime, it was not terror but euphoria that was the leading emotion in those days of March 1933. A massive propaganda campaign convinced the German public that this was the long awaited moment of national renewal and rebirth (*Nationale Erhebung*, national uprising). The position of Joseph Goebbels was formalised on 13 March 1933 by his appointment as Minister for Propaganda and Popular

A poster from 1932. The organised will of the nation.

Enlightenment. He now had complete control of press, radio and all other means of public communication. Relentlessly the theme was hammered home that after fourteen years of humiliation and disaster Germany was now heading for a bright future under its glorious leader, Adolf Hitler. The Führer was portrayed as a national hero in a line stretching back through Bismarck to Frederick the Great. On 21 March the newly elected Reichstag had its formal opening with a service in the garrison church at Potsdam, a shrine of the Prussian military tradition. This 'Day of Potsdam' was cleverly organised by Goebbels to convince all nationally-minded Germans that Hitler and his regime deserved their full support. Hitler, in formal civilian morning coat, with top hat, bowed deeply in front of Hindenburg, in the uniform of an imperial field marshal. Two days later the Reichstag met for its first business session. The meeting place, an opera house, since the Reichstag building was a burnt out shell, was surrounded by stormtroopers baying for blood. The remaining deputies of the republican parties could not be sure of escaping with their lives. The Reichstag passed the Enabling Act, surrendering its power to make law to the Chancellor and his Cabinet for four years. The legal side of the Nazi take-over was thereby completed and the signature of the President for decrees under article 48 was no longer required. Only the SPD voted against the Enabling Act and Hitler, having first played the sober statesman, then rounded on them violently, calling them the rotten and dead representatives of an age now past.

Gleichschaltung

In the next few weeks there was a rapid process of Nazification of all the many organisations and structures that existed in German society as in all modern developed societies. The process was called *Gleichschaltung,* which can be roughly translated as alignment. It usually meant that active members of the Nazi Party were appointed to key positions, while members of the republican parties or Jews were dismissed. Only a few of the major steps in this take-over of all aspects of a nation's existence can be mentioned here. On 1 April a boycott of Jewish shops all over Germany was announced. It was a response, typical of the Nazi regime, to the adverse comments in the foreign press on events in Germany, and in particular on the anti-Semitic measures. The German Jews were to be held hostage, so that the Western press would hold its fire. The boycott was not popular with the German public, who mostly resented being kept out of Jewish-owned department stores. While few Germans helped their Jewish fellow-citizens, anti-Semitism appealed more to the fully committed Nazis than to the wider public. After a few days the boycott was called off, but on 7 April a law was published under which Jews, or non-Aryans, as they were now called, and politically unreliable persons could be excluded from the civil service. It was the first step to the establishment of a racial state

- *Gleichschaltung*

and flew in the face of all ideas of the rule of law, and equality before the law, as hitherto understood in most civilised countries. The law of 7 April was only slightly modified under pressure from Hindenburg, who had otherwise remained unresponsive to appeals that he should move against Nazi excesses. Jews who had served as front-line soldiers in the First World War were for the moment exempt from the law.

Unfortunately, the great majority of the German people cared little about the loss of freedom and were much more concerned to jump on to the Nazi bandwagon as swiftly as possible. Members of the old democratic parties were leaving them in droves and so many were queuing up to join the NSDAP that in May 1933 a temporary block on new members was enforced.

On 1 May 1933 the new regime celebrated Labour Day in great style, to show that the Nazi party was truly a workers' party. Hitler made a speech invoking the blessings of the almighty on the newly risen German people. The following day squads of stormtroopers turned up at trade union buildings all over Germany, arrested officials and ransacked files. The free trade union movement, one of the most powerful in Europe, was smashed and there was no resistance. It was perhaps the most stunning single episode in the dynamic, brutal Nazi drive for power and for the annihilation of their opponents. In the next few weeks all political parties other than the Nazi Party ceased to exist. They had all deluded themselves that they could somehow survive this avalanche. On the left many still clung for a time to the Marxist notion that Hitler's rule could not last long and would inevitably collapse. On the right the DNVP and the *Stahlhelm* had seen themselves as the allies and the 'tamers' of the Nazis, but were forced out of existence when they had served their purpose. Hugenberg resigned from the government. On 14 July the NSDAP was declared the sole German party.

Economic Recovery

It was a political revolution, the great counter-revolution, as Goebbels styled it, against the ideas and values of the French Revolution of 1789. Most of Germany's leading writers, journalists and intellectuals were forced into exile, their books were ceremonially burnt and excluded from libraries, and even many of her most famous scientists left. The Nazi take-over was not a social and economic revolution to the same extent that it was a political, ideological and cultural one. Hitler knew that it was vital to the consolidation of his regime that there should be an improvement in the economic situation as rapidly as possible. Too much of a disturbance of business and industry, such as the more revolutionary elements in the Nazi Party would have liked, would therefore have to be avoided and in fact the basis of the capitalist market system, the private ownership of industry, was never changed throughout the twelve years of the Third Reich.

Table 7.2: German unemployment, 1928-37

	Officially registered figures, average p.a.	*Per cent of dependent earners*
1928	1.4 million	6.3
1929	1.9 million	8.5
1930	3.1 million	14.0
1931	4.5 million	21.9
1932	5.6 million	29.9
1933	4.8 million	25.9
1934	2.7 million	13.5
1935	2.2 million	10.3
1936	1.6 million	7.4
1937	0.9 million	4.1

Nevertheless, business and industry experienced *Gleichschaltung,* like all other aspects of German life, and it was clear from the beginning that it would have to conform to the political aims of the new masters. Firms were forced to find positions for Nazi activists or promote them. In general business, large or small, had every reason to welcome the new regime, for it provided stability and the basis for economic recovery. It got rid of the trade unions and the left-wing parties, the natural opponents of the business community.

Hitler was fortunate that at the moment when he came to power the low point of the depression had been passed and the mild measures of reflation initiated by the Papen and Schleicher governments were beginning to take effect. These measures were, however, reinforced both by making more credit available and by direct steps creating employment. A well-known example is the Autobahn building programme, for which plans existed from the Weimar period, but which was now put into operation with a great propaganda flourish. Hitler himself cut the first turf and there was a great parade of labour service battalions, still voluntary, but later to become compulsory. There was much talk of winning 'the battle of employment' and the generation of economic optimism had a high priority. Contrary to what is often said, the Autobahn programme had initially no military-strategic purpose, but in internal discussions Hitler emphasised from the beginning that work-creation must contribute to the future military build-up.

A programme which clearly had a dual purpose was the granting of loans to couples entering upon marriage. Repayments were reduced when children were born. In the year 1933 200,000 more marriages were entered into than the year before. It was a way of getting women off the labour market and raising the birthrate, a matter of particular concern to the race ideology of the Nazis. Although unemployment remained high in the first two years after Hitler came to power, there was enough of an improvement to reconcile even many working-class people and former supporters of the left-wing parties to the regime. The loss of freedom and of their trade union rights and the fixing of their wages by Nazi labour trustees, as they were called, was outweighed for many by a return to employment. The Social Democrat leaders now in exile had to recognise in their reports, based on a good network of underground information and still an important source for historians, that the new regime had managed to gain a degree of acceptance among German workers.

The man increasingly entrusted by Hitler with the management of the economy was Dr Schacht, who returned to the position of President of the Reichsbank, the central German bank, from which he had resigned in March 1930, three years later. Schacht had been credited with the introduction of the new currency in 1923 and was well known in international banking and business circles. His presence in a leading position after the Nazi take-over reassured the business community inside and outside Germany. Schacht was willing to reactivate the German economy by credit-creation. In particular he instituted a system of bills of exchange called Mefo, short for *Metallurgische Forschungsgesellschaft*, discountable by the Reichsbank, through which major firms could be paid for their armaments deliveries while, at the same time, the real purpose of the payments, for purposes prohibited by the Versailles Treaty, could be kept hidden.

A Disguised Revolution

By the summer of 1933 Hitler could declare that the Nazi revolution had been successful all along the line, but that the moment of consolidation had arrived. He himself was astonished at the ease with which it had all been done and at the almost total lack of resistance.

- The three crucial elements in the Nazi take-over had been legality, terror and deception.
- The formal legality of Hitler's appointment as chancellor and of the subsequent steps to acquire dictatorial power, such as the Enabling Act, meant that the whole state apparatus fell without resistance into Nazi hands.
- From the elites at the top, the Reichswehr generals, the senior civil servants, the major industrialists, through the middle layers down to the rank and file the majority had not only no reason to oppose the take-over, but mostly welcomed it enthusiastically.
- This was where the element of deception came in, the myth that this was a national renewal in which all right-minded Germans should participate. For most people the radical, revolutionary purpose of National Socialism was well hidden.

- Hitler took great care to appear personally as the moderate responsible statesman and only on rare occasions did he show himself in his true colours.
- But just in case there was any back-sliding, there was the reign of terror unleashed, with official connivance, by the SA against those clearly marked out on political or racial grounds as opponents of the regime. Increasingly, the terror on the streets was supplemented by official repression.
- The first official concentration camp was established at Dachau, north of Munich in March 1933.

The SA and a 'Second Revolution'

The dynamic force with which the brown flood of Nazism had washed over Germany could not disguise the fact that many of the existing structures had survived and were indeed essential to the continued functioning of life. This was clearly so in the economic sphere, but another area, the armed forces, vital to Hitler's plans for conquest, had hardly been touched by the Nazis. As we have seen, the acquiescence of the Reichswehr was essential to the formation of the Hitler Cabinet in January 1933 and sealed by the replacement of Schleicher by Blomberg as Minister of Defence. Blomberg and his Chief of Staff, Colonel von Reichenau, were, like all German senior officers, dedicated to the restoration of Germany as a great power through the rebuilding of a powerful army. They became convinced that close co-operation with Hitler was the best way of achieving their goal. They had, however, a rival in the SA, a part-time army, but with about three million members by 1933 many times outnumbering the Reichswehr still limited to 100,000 men. The Chief of Staff of the SA was Ernst Röhm, a man who as a Bavarian regular officer had given a great deal of assistance to Hitler in his early Munich days. He and his fellow SA leaders saw their force as the revolutionary army of National Socialism. Like the armies of the French Revolution, they would carry the revolution all over the world. They were suspicious of the way in which Hitler had apparently compromised with all the traditional forces in German society, most obviously the mainly aristocratic generals of the Reichswehr.

As the Nazi political take-over swiftly reached its goal in the summer of 1933, Hitler, conscious of the need for stability particularly in the economic sphere, declared the revolution at an end. The SA was thus left without an obvious function, many of its old fighters disappointed both by the public and personal outcome of the changes. There was talk of a second revolution and Röhm gave encouragement to such ideas in public and in private. Ceaseless meetings, rallies and demonstrations showed the SA burning for further action. In the autumn and winter of 1933/34 there was growing tension between the SA and the Reichswehr, over training, the

availability of arms and of money. The army leaders were desperately concerned to preserve their monopoly as bearers of arms. Hitler, as was his wont in such situations, kept aloof from the conflict. Ultimately, he could not challenge the Army and it was essential to his plans to destroy the Versailles system and conquer living space. On the other hand, he shared the aims of his rough-neck SA fighters and they had played an essential role in his revolution. He did not want to be at the mercy of the conservative forces with whose co-operation his rule had been established.

The Night of the Long Knives

A last-ditch attempt by such conservatives, whose plans to 'tame' Hitler had failed so lamentably, to reassert their influence brought matters to a head in June 1934. By this time Hindenburg was not expected to live much longer, but while he was still there an attempt to limit Hitler's power and restore something of the rule of law had a chance of success. On 17 June 1934 Papen delivered a speech at Marburg, criticising the violence, lawlessness and corruption in the Nazi regime. Hitler realised that his position was now threatened not only by Röhm's loud-mouthed refusal to accept a subordinate position for the SA, but by a move to restore the monarchy after Hindenburg's death. Göring had allied himself with Himmler, whose blackshirt SS, already 30,000 strong, represented a rising power in the regime, determined to cut down their rival Röhm. On 28 June, to put everybody off the scent, Hitler went to the Rhineland, to attend the wedding of a Gauleiter and to inspect factories. He had ordered Röhm to command his senior SA leaders to join him at a spa, Bad Wiessee, 30 miles south of Munich, where the SA Chief of Staff was taking a cure. During the night of 29 to 30 June Hitler flew to Munich and then arrested Röhm in his hotel. Other SA leaders were arrested as they travelled to the meeting at Bad Wiessee and then executed. Röhm was given the option of committing suicide before being shot. In the meantime, Göring had initiated the purge in Berlin and other cities. Many SA leaders were shot, but also several members of Papen's entourage and the Vice-Chancellor himself was put under house arrest. Schleicher and his wife were shot by an SS hit squad and so was his former assistant General von Bredow. Many old scores were settled and among those murdered were Gregor Strasser and Gustav von Kahr, the man who had crushed the beer hall putsch in 1923. Altogether the number of dead probably reached into three figures.

The great beneficiary of these murderous events, which the foreign press named the Night of the Long Knives, was Hitler himself. Five weeks later, on 2 August 1934, Hindenburg died and Hitler succeeded him as head of state, combining the offices of chancellor and president, with the title Führer and Chancellor. The Reichswehr swore an oath to him personally as the new commander-in-chief, which became a pretext for those generals who later refused to join any plot to remove him. The

Reichswehr, soon to become the Wehrmacht, was deeply compromised by these events. It had given logistic support to the SS hit squads carrying out the purge and had condoned the murder of two of its senior officers. Hitler's stock rose further among the population at large. It was believed that he had acted decisively against the most radical and corrupt elements in National Socialism. Much was made of the fact that Röhm and some of his entourage were homosexuals, something that had never previously deterred Hitler from associating with them. Hitler's claim that he had crushed a plot against the state and that he had been forced to become 'the supreme justiciar of the German people' was widely believed in Germany. Even before 30 June 1934 Hitler's popular position was such that the contending forces could only move when they knew him to be on their side. Soon, reinforced by his foreign policy successes, he became the integrating figure, the Messiah, around whom the Third Reich was built. Abroad, the Röhm purge was more realistically assessed. It was widely realised that a great power in the centre of Europe was now ruled by a gangster-like regime that would stop at nothing. Unfortunately, few consequences were drawn from this realisation, which soon faded again.

Hitler as Dictator

Hitler now combined in his hands a degree of power rare in modern history, unique for a large, highly complex and advanced society like Germany. He could issue orders (variously labelled *Führerbefehle, Führererlasse, Führerverordnungen*), but he could also issue formal legislation, since the Enabling Act had vested the power in him and the Cabinet. The latter ceased to be a body for consultation and met increasingly rarely, for the last time in 1938. This way of governing meant that the normal system of law, sometimes called normative, which is essential to the running of normal, orderly governments, was increasingly bypassed or superseded by the exercise of arbitrary power by men like Himmler, the SS Chief, armed by an order from Hitler. The Führer knew that such men, totally loyal to him, would carry out his most radical intentions, while he could still appear as moderate and aloof. Many of the most extreme and criminal activities of the Third Reich, such as the euthanasia campaign to kill the mentally and physically handicapped and the murder of most of Europe's Jews in the Holocaust were carried out, usually in secrecy, in this way. When Germany acquired control of most of Europe during the war, those governing the areas outside the Reich proper also derived their authority direct from Hitler. Such a system, if one can call it that, could release great energies, mostly of a destructive kind, but it also led to chaos, confusion and disintegration, particularly when in the later years of the war Hitler's Reich was careering towards defeat.

From 1934 onwards Hitler himself increasingly withdrew from regular contact with the machinery of government. He despised bureaucrats and lawyers, who he felt strangled the vital forces of the nation, so important in his social-Darwinist view of the world. While Hindenburg was still alive he tried to make himself look like an ordinary chancellor, attending to the affairs of his office. Thereafter he spent less and less time in Berlin. He moved about restlessly, attending rallies, ceremonies and demonstrations. He spent more of his time in his mountain hide-out in Berchtesgaden, some 80 miles southeast of Munich, renamed the Berghof, and only those officials and ministers he wanted to see had access to him there. He empowered competing subordinates to act in the same sphere of activity. Thus, in the area of foreign policy, a field in which the Führer took a special interest, the Reich foreign office (*Auswärtiges Amt*) found itself undercut by special assignments given to Ribbentrop, later foreign minister, and by Alfred Rosenberg, the party ideologue. In the economic sphere Göring was a rival of Schacht. Frequently Hitler himself shunned decisions, letting his subordinates fight it out. Again this conformed to his social-Darwinist outlook on life. Some historians have for this reason called him a 'weak dictator', for he did indeed allow many matters to drift, refusing to get involved.

Interpretations of the Third Reich

- Historians have had to modify the view, which the Nazis themselves emphasised, that the Third Reich was a tightly organised totalitarian state.
- They have instead called the Nazi regime a 'polycracy', a state split into many rival empires.
- Neither the description of Hitler as a weak dictator nor that of his regime as a polycracy is wholly accurate.
- Hitler could always get his way when he wanted to but distanced himself from anything damaging to his personal popularity.
- It was precisely because he was not enmeshed in bureaucracy that he could take key decisions without any interference or control and could drive the Third Reich to the crimes and excesses for which it became notorious.
- The confusion of competing empires did not stop the Third Reich from becoming a progressively more totalitarian society, where the citizen was no longer a private individual, but controlled in all aspects of his life by the ruling regime and its ideology.

Related to the controversy whether Hitler was a weak or strong dictator and how far an analysis of the Third Reich should centre on Hitler are the differences of interpretation that have been labelled 'intentionalist' and 'structuralist'. Many of the most central aspects of the Third Reich, the war of conquest to acquire Lebensraum and the setting up of a racial state, involving the annihilation of inferior beings, such as Jews, gypsies and the mentally and physically handicapped, as well as the reduction to virtual slavery of inferior races like the Slavs, were part of the Nazi ideology and of Hitler's own views. That they occurred was therefore 'intentional'. But the way they happened also owed much to the 'structure of things'. Initially the Nazi regime had to operate within the confines of the German state and society which it increasingly took over, penetrated and finally disintegrated. The unco-ordinated way of Hitler's manner of governing meant that policies developed out of the interplay of forces and opportunities. Even the murder of European Jews, the Holocaust, started to some extent from the bottom up. The technique of mass killing in gas chambers which had been tested in the euthanasia campaign, the killing of the handicapped, emerged from below as the most efficient method of mass murder. It was, however, all initiated and driven on by Hitler himself, the other major Nazi leaders around him and by the thrust of the Nazi ideology.

The Beginnings of Hitler's Foreign Policy

The first stages of Hitler's foreign policy show the same confusing interplay of continuity, revolutionary change and deliberate deception to obscure the true intention of the regime that had marked the domestic take-over. On the surface all was continuity. The same professional diplomat of conservative-nationalist views, von Neurath, who had been Foreign Minister in the Papen and Schleicher Cabinets, continued to serve. Along with the presence of Blomberg as Defence Minister it seemed to indicate that the real power would be in traditional hands. Hitler knew that there was a zone of risk he had to cross in foreign affairs, before Germany was sufficiently rearmed, and the impression of continuity served his purpose well. In 1933 the first steps of open defiance of the Versailles Treaty were accompanied by a propaganda barrage professing devotion to peace. On 17 May 1933 he issued a great peace appeal in the Reichstag, which even the SPD, within days of its own total extinction, felt compelled to vote for. In private Hitler talked a different language. During his first week as chancellor he addressed a meeting of generals assembled in the private flat of the Commander-in-Chief of the Army. He told them that he would again make the German people bearers of arms, by eradicating all traces of Marxism and pacificism. He opened up vistas of future expansion, particularly in Eastern Europe. To some extent he told the generals what they wanted to hear, illustrating how difficult it was for German nationalists to distinguish between what they wanted and the much more radical and revolutionary aims of National Socialism.

While Hitler covered his tracks in foreign policy, he also started to develop agencies alternative to the official diplomatic machinery. Rosenberg and more significantly, Ribbentrop, who had impressed Hitler by his knowledge of foreign countries and languages, took on special assignments. By the autumn of 1933 Hitler was ready for a more open gesture of defiance of the existing system. He left the League of Nations, thereby showing that he regarded all the attempts to establish a peaceful world, which had so much dominated the thinking of all people of good intent, as a complete waste of time. This step he submitted to a plebiscite of the German people, the first time this way of showing the apparent solidarity of the whole nation behind its Führer was brought into play. There was a yes-vote of well over 90 per cent. Hitler thus proceeded by methods with which the established system of relations between the powers was simply unable to cope. Propaganda smoke screens and plain deception, willingness to use agreements and treaties simply as tactical devices, to be discarded at any time, everywhere confused the diplomats, politicians and public, who expected at least a minimum of trust. Much of the Versailles system had already been discarded or weakened and Hitler's battering ram soon destroyed what was left.

Questions to Consider

- What role did legality, terror and deception play in the Nazi take-over?
- Why was the take-over accomplished with such ease?
- Why was there no major immediate social and economic change?
- What was the notion of a 'Second Revolution'?
- How did the Night of the Long Knives strengthen Hitler's position?

EXAMINATION QUESTIONS

1. Why was Hitler able to establish a Nazi dictatorship so quickly after becoming Chancellor in January 1933?
2. 'After 1933 only the SA and the German Army stood in the way of complete power for Hitler.' Is this statement correct and how did Hitler deal with these organisations?
3. Why was there not more resistance to the Nazi establishment of power in the years 1933-5?

8 The Third Reich

Life in the Third Reich

Historians have doubted if there was ever a point where the Nazi regime was sufficiently static to merit the label 'system'. As we have seen, Hitler's rule relied so much on sheer actionism that it never had a chance of reaching any kind of plateau. If there were years, however, when there was something that one could call normality for the Third Reich it was the time between late 1934 and early 1938. During that time the Nazis attempted to turn their state, initially based on a compromise with existing structures, elites and procedures, into the totalitarian society envisaged by their ideology. There would no longer be individual private citizens, but *Volksgenossen* (people's comrades) whose only existence would be within and through the state based on race. As with the other major totalitarian system of the twentieth century, the Communist system, human nature itself would be reconstructed. This at any rate was the aim of Hitler's regime, even if it was never completely achieved.

Youth and Education

Such an undertaking had to start with the young. It had been one of the advantages of National Socialism before 1933 that it was perceived to be, and was more than the other parties, a movement of youth. Even so the party's youth wing, the Hitler Youth, was only about 100,000 strong in 1933, but by the time war broke out membership had become compulsory and it had nearly nine million members. Boys from 10 to 14 entered the *Jungvolk* and from 15 to 18 were in the Hitler Youth (*Hitlerjugend*) proper. The equivalent formations for girls were *Jungmädel* and *Bund Deutscher Mädel*. The motto of the Hitler Youth was 'Führer command - we obey'. There were constant roll calls, indoctrination sessions, sport, camps, for boys military training. Other youth organisations, such as those of the Church's, were unable to continue their work. The Hitler Youth undoubtedly appealed to the sense of adventure of many young people and built on their natural desire to get away from their parents and elders and assert their independence. It thereby withdrew them from home influences that might have stood in the way of Nazi indoctrination. It prepared boys to become the soldiers of the Third Reich. As war approached, there were signs that this massive programme of regimentation was arousing some resistance and alienation among the young. Jazz, the pop music of the day, was, for example, banned because it was of Negro origin, but the regime found it increasingly difficult to prevent the young from listening and dancing to it.

Schools and universities had to conform to Nazi ideology in their teaching and in all subjects new curricula and textbooks were introduced. The anti-intellectual, anti-rational thrust of the ideology meant that there was a marked decline in standards. Book-learning was treated with contempt. Universities experienced a decline in student numbers, particularly of women, because the Nazi ideology, relegating them to a domestic role and to becoming producers of soldiers, left them with few professional openings. Some fields, for example atomic physics, where Germany had held a leading place, were regarded as having been overwhelmed by Jewish influence and were severely hampered, some of their most distinguished practitioners, like Albert Einstein, having been forced into exile on racial and political grounds. It was one of the reasons why Germany failed to develop an atomic bomb during the war. While traditional methods and institutions of education languished, various new institutions were established to produce the elite for the Nazi racial state. The most conspicuous of these were called *Ordensburgen,* built like medieval knightly castles, whose inmates, Junkers or knight cadets, were indoctrinated to perform their role as totally dedicated soldiers of the Führer.

Control of the Workers

Once entered upon the adult world the *Volksgenosse* was subjected to regimentation and control in all aspects of his working life and his leisure. The working man, for example, instead of belonging to a trade union, now belonged to the *Deutsche Arbeitsfront* (German Labour Front), which regulated his wages and working conditions. It had a leisure organisation called *Kraft durch Freude* (Strength through Joy), which organised holidays and other leisure activities. The DAF, headed by Robert Ley, was one of the major empires of the Nazi state and it had some success in making the German working class feel that there was now greater equality of opportunity and of esteem in the Nazi *Volksgemeinschaft* than there had been in the individualist, class-based society of the past. One of the schemes promoted by the KdF was saving for a car, something that workers had never been able to aspire to before. The car, the Volkswagen, was designed, but never became available to German consumers during the Nazi period. The savings scheme was merely a way of syphoning off excess purchasing power in an increasingly inflationary situation and the car was manufactured for the armed forces only.

Control of the Media and of Culture

Professional men, lawyers, doctors, were equally regimented. The whole field of culture, for example, was controlled by a Reich Culture Chamber, with sub-chambers for writers, musicians and so on, and was part of the empire established by Goebbels. Nobody could write, publish or play unless a member of one of these chambers, and anybody not politically or racially reliable was excluded. The Press was minutely controlled and Goebbels' Propaganda Ministry issued exact guidelines on how all issues of any importance were to be handled. Avant-garde, experimental art was frowned upon and labelled 'degenerate'. Goebbels mounted an exhibition in Munich in 1937, called 'Degenerate Art', in which paintings of many of Germany's most distinguished painters, many of them by then in exile, were displayed. Fear and incomprehension of what was new, among the ordinary public, was used to persuade people that National Socialism had freed them from some kind of cultural sickness. In contrast the highly representational painting of Aryan heroes and peasants and the monumental architecture favoured by Hitler were declared to be a sign of national health.

For all Germans life in the Third Reich was punctuated by officially decreed festivities, rallies and mass demonstrations, the annual party rally, Hitler's birthday, the day of German Culture, the day of the German Craftsman, and so on. Some of these were great pageants, staged around Hitler himself, of which the 'Cathedral of Light', the use of massed searchlights at the Nuremberg party rally, organised by Albert Speer, Hitler's architect, was a striking example. It has been called the 'aestheticising of politics' and it impressed many people, even many foreigners. The Hitler regime appeared to have found a way of manipulating and controlling the masses and instilling them with its own sense of purpose. No amount of pageantry and manipulation would have worked, had there not been some solid foundation for the growing triumphalism of the Nazis. The foundation came from the early economic improvement, modest enough until fuelled by rearmament, and then from the apparently sensational success of Hitler's foreign policy from 1935 on. There was, under the surface, a good deal of grumbling and discontent, but it was rarely directed against Hitler himself and his policies, but against the lesser Nazi bosses, often corrupt, incompetent and downright vicious. When there were complaints and grumbles, it was usually accompanied by the words 'if only the Führer knew', such was the almost god-like standing Hitler had with most Germans.

- There was a reverse side to the picture showing the German people marching in serried ranks saluting their Führer.
- It was the utter isolation of the individual human being, ironical in a society that put so much stress on community and solidarity.

- Only when the *Volksgenosse* closed his front door behind him could he retain any identity as a person and gain some respite from the ceaseless propaganda of the regime.
- Even then he or she could not be sure that their children, indoctrinated in the Hitler Youth, might not inform against them.
- In the middle 1930s Germany was therefore becoming an increasingly totalitarian society.
- A few safety valves were left. Light entertainment, escapist films, popular literature and music continued to flourish and provided some distraction from the relentless demands of the regime and its propaganda.

The Hitler Myth

- The Hitler myth, more than the Nazi ideology, is the integrating factor in the Third Reich. The myth was largely created by the Goebbels' propaganda machine.
- Ordinary Germans saw Hitler as successful, first on the economy, then in foreign policy. Reversing Versailles was a universally accepted aim, but war was feared.
- When war came, Hitler was again, until 1941, sensationally successful.
- When failure loomed, many Germans found it difficult to 'say goodbye to the Führer'. All alternatives had been eliminated, and consciousness of the atrocities committed, particularly in the East, made everybody fearful of the revenge that would be exacted when defeat came.

The System of Terror

Terror was, as we have seen, an essential factor in the establishment of the Nazi regime in its early months. It was then brought increasingly under official control, but remained a necessary backstop in the consolidation of this totalitarian society. Heinrich Himmler became the central figure in the administration of terror, the head of yet another Nazi empire, eventually the most powerful of them all (see page 19). Himmler's SS (*Schutz Staffel,* originally Hitler's personal bodyguard) played a vital role in the Night of the Long Knives and then replaced the SA as the army of National Socialism. By 1936 Himmler was in control of the three main elements of his power, the SS, the police and the concentration camps. Part of the police was the Gestapo (short for *Geheime Staatspolizei,* Secret State Police), which had the function of rendering harmless potential enemies of the regime. It was run by Himmler's principal lieutenant, Reinhard Heydrich. Covered by the special orders from the Führer, Himmler's security apparatus could cut through all ordinary processes of law.

The existence of the concentration camps, and the brutal treatment meted out to their inmates by the SS, was well known to the ordinary

German public, though the pretence was kept up that only anti-social and anti-state elements were sent there. Although the numbers confined in concentration camps during the more stable years of the Nazi regime had dropped, reaching a low point of about 10,000 in 1937, Hitler resisted attempts to do away with the system and its deterrent effect was maintained. Dachau, the original official camp, held mainly political detainees, while the two other major camps operating in the middle 1930s, Sachsenhausen and Buchenwald, were for prisoners whom the regime wanted especially to exclude from the Volksgemeinschaft and who would not have been found guilty under the ordinary law. By 1937 Himmler had in place a security apparatus that could effectively spy on the whole population and quickly trace any source of disaffection and opposition. Modern research has shown that the Gestapo relied heavily on information from the ordinary public, often motivated by personal vendettas. Terror was so effective, because the regime commanded increasing support among the majority of Germans. Once Hitler embarked upon territorial expansion in 1938, the system of terror and concentration camps expanded hugely and became ever more extreme, culminating from 1941 in the notorious death camps, like Auschwitz, Treblinka and Sobibor in occupied Poland. In peace-time Nazi Germany it was only the declared enemies of National Socialism who felt the full force of the terror, but about a million Germans passed through the camps between 1933 and 1939.

The Racial State

The establishment of a racial state, the full horror of which only became evident during the war, began in the early days of the Third Reich. As we have seen (see page 87), the Law for the Restoration of the Professional Civil Service, of 7 April 1933, had already given legal force to discrimination on racial grounds. Among the spate of Nazi legislation promulgated on 14 July 1933 there was a Law for the Prevention of Hereditarily Diseased Progeny, under which compulsory sterilisation became possible. An amendment of November 1935 made abortion up to the sixth month of pregnancy legal. About 200,000 sterilisations of women were carried out between 1933 and 1945, about 1 per cent of women of child-bearing age. Altogether about 350,000 to 400,000 sterilisations were carried out, mostly before 1939, when the euthanasia campaign, already mentioned (see page 95), took over.

This campaign started when a couple petitioned Hitler in the winter of 1938/39 to allow their deformed child to be killed. In October 1939 Hitler signed a note, which he symbolically backdated to 1 September 1939, the date of the outbreak of war, authorising officials in his party chancellery to arrange the killing of incurably diseased persons. From this the campaign developed, leading to the death of some 70,000 persons. The euthanasia campaign could not, in the longer run, remain hidden and started to cause unrest at the height of the war. It was temporarily suspended after an outspoken sermon against it by the Catholic Bishop, Count von Galen of Münster in August 1941, but it was soon resumed in a more carefully concealed way. Even the temporary suspension suggests that the regime was very concerned to avoid anything unpopular or damaging to morale, and that therefore other crimes, such as the murder of Jews, could have been stopped, at least in Germany, if more people had spoken out against them. Hitler and his henchmen learnt two lessons from the euthanasia campaign: the Führer never again associated himself in so direct a manner with large-scale extermination, such as the Holocaust, by any signed order; and the technique of killing people in gas chambers was first tried out in the euthanasia campaign.

Another early move of the Nazi regime was against people labelled anti-social. This fitted in well with the image the Third Reich wanted to give itself in the eyes of the majority, as a society in which law and order were preserved, crime reduced to a minimum and decency upheld. In the course of a campaign against begging in 1933 about 100,000 beggars were temporarily incarcerated, often in the 'wild' concentration camps established by the SA, but then mostly released again. In November 1933 a Law against Dangerous Habitual Criminals was passed, which enabled the police to put people with two or more criminal convictions in unlimited 'preventive detention'. Criminal-biological investigations could be carried out in prisons from 1935 onwards and could lead to compulsory sterilisation. By 1937 Himmler, as Head of SS and Security Services, had got a grip on this area and a circular of December 1937 gave a definition of who was to be regarded as anti-social and work-shy. In April 1938 a Reich campaign against the work-shy was mounted, during which Heydrich ordered each regional police district to make a quota of 200 arrests. Gypsies suffered a holocaust of their own, some 200,000 of them being eventually murdered in Nazi occupied territory. Homosexuals were severely persecuted and had their own distinguishing mark, a pink triangle, in the concentration camps. Homosexuality was a crime in Germany long before the Third Reich, as it was then in most countries, but the Nazis made the legislation against it much more stringent. In most of their racial and persecutions and exterminations the Nazis were in fact able to build on existing attitudes. At least since the end of the nineteenth century there was a preoccupation with 'racial health' in many countries, spurred by the theories of Darwin. Even in Britain there was a eugenics movement, motivated by the perception that the quality of the race was deteriorating, because the 'best' elements in society seemed to have the lowest birthrate. In the National Socialist ideology such ideas held a central place and were then put into practice with all the traditional restraints removed.

The Persecution of the Jews

The Jews were the greatest enemy to be eliminated from the Nazi racial state. Without a country of their own, they were parasites on all other races, particularly on the Germanic Aryan race. They were also the great ideological enemy, being responsible for liberalism, humanism, pacificism, Bolshevism, socialism and even Christianity. In practice the Hitler regime had to step somewhat carefully in implementing its anti-Jewish plans. As we have seen (page 87) the boycott against Jewish shops on 1 April 1933 almost backfired. Nevertheless, the exclusion of Jews from all aspects of German life went on relentlessly. It was not given a high profile, but it furthered what was then the main aim of Nazi anti-Semitism, to force the Jews to emigrate from Germany. In fact by the outbreak of war only about a third of the half million Jews in Germany were left. In the early years of the Third Reich Jews were not only forced out of all official positions, such as the civil service and the judiciary, but also their position in the professions became increasingly precarious. Jewish lawyers and doctors were confined to Jewish clients and patients. They were completely excluded from the media and from cultural life, in which many Jews had played a distinguished role before 1933. The only area where they could still work to some extent was business and commerce. The regime could not afford to disturb the process of economic recovery and Schacht, the economic overlord in those years, did not want to offend foreign opinion. All the indications are that there were always plenty of people willing to profit from the removal of Jewish competitors in the professions. When

The sign reads 'The Jews are our misfortune'. *From a Nazi children's book*

Schacht's influence declined after 1936, the 'Aryanisation' of Jewish businesses gathered pace.

The Nuremberg Laws

The slow and relatively orderly exclusion of Jews was, however, not enough for the more rabid and revolutionary elements among Nazi activists, for whom anti-Semitism was a kind of barometer indicating the progress of their revolution. The most rabid Jew-baiter in the NSDAP was Julius Streicher, the Gauleiter of Franconia, a thoroughly disreputable character. He published a pornographic anti-Semitic paper *Der Stürmer,* which was displayed in many public places. Hitler was thus not averse to stoking anti-Semitism from below, but he was careful not to connect himself personally too openly with such campaigns. In 1935 anti-Semitic activism from below was again gathering pace. It was partly the result of the set-back many Nazi old fighters had suffered in the Night of the Long Knives; partly it arose from a growing Nazi triumphalism, engendered by Hitler's early foreign policy successes. Hitler, having allowed things to come to the boil from below, suddenly and at short notice pounced at the Nuremberg party rally in September 1935. The notorious Nuremberg Laws were announced forbidding marriages and sexual intercourse between Aryans and non-Aryans and the employment of Aryan servants in Jewish households. The full absurdity of Nazi racialism is demonstrated by the fact that the only way in which a full Aryan could be defined was by a religious criterion, namely he or she had to have four grandparents none of whom professed the Jewish religion. Someone who had two Jewish grandparents was classified as a half-Aryan. Many people believed Hitler's declaration that the 'Jewish question' was now finally and legally settled. It was another example of the illusions widely held about the true nature of Nazism and its leader. With the Nuremberg Laws Hitler had in fact indicated to his old fighters that he was still the true Nazi revolutionary to whom they had given their loyalty. There was also an implied warning to the many nationalist-conservative elements remaining in the bureaucracy and judiciary that no backsliding in the implementation of the Nazi ideology would be tolerated.

The Pogrom of November 1938

After the Nuremberg Laws anti-Semitic measures for a time resumed their low profile. Even the more conspicuous *Stürmer* display cabinets were removed when, in 1936, many foreign visitors came to Germany for the Olympic Games. The persecution of the Jews turned violent again in 1938. Nazi triumphalism reached new heights after the bloodless acquisition of Austria in March and the Sudetenland in September. Foreign opinion could now be deliberately outraged. The acquisition of new territories also increased again the number of Jews under German control and when

German troops entered Vienna particularly violent attacks on Jews took place. The murder of a German diplomat in Paris in November 1938, by a Polish Jew outraged by the expulsion of his parents from Germany, gave the excuse for an anti-Jewish pogrom. During the night of 9/10 November synagogues all over Germany were burnt down, Jewish shops smashed, hence the term *Kristallnacht* (night of the broken glass) and some 30,000 Jewish men were sent to concentration camps. It was said to be the result of popular indignation boiling over, but in fact it was stoked from below by Nazi local bosses and then co-ordinated from above. Goebbels and Hitler were assembled in Munich for the annual anniversary celebrations of the Beer Hall Putsch. Goebbels, at this time out of favour because of an affair with a Czech actress, took the lead, hoping to regain lost ground, thereby enabling Hitler again to distance himself personally. It was soon obvious that the action, far from being the result of popular indignation, was not popular among the order-loving German public. It also caused a rapid evaporation of the euphoria following the peaceful settlement of the Sudeten crisis in Britain and other countries. For German Jews it at last became clear that there was no future for them in the country in which their forebears had lived for more than a thousand years. Those taken to concentration camps had to undertake to emigrate as soon as possible on their release. Those remaining in Germany were eventually to meet their deaths in the extermination camps of Eastern Europe. The persecution and final extermination of Jews was always the logical result of Hitler's intentions, but was by no means precisely planned, any more than the other aspects of the Nazi take-over and their wars of conquest.

The Resistance

After the collapse of the Third Reich much attention was devoted to the resistance against the regime. Faced with the crimes committed by the Nazi regime in their name, most Germans claimed that organised resistance was impossible once Hitler was in power. In the first few weeks after 30 January 1933 it might have had a chance, but the mixture of legality, nationalist euphoria and terror, with which Hitler orchestrated his take-over was, as we have seen, extremely effective in keeping his potential opponents confused. The SPD leaders believed that if they stuck to a strictly legal course the party could survive, just as it had survived a period of repression under Bismarck in the 1880s. When by early summer 1933 this had proved a total delusion, there was little the main SPD leaders could do other than go into exile. The party was reconstituted as Sopade (*Sozialdemokratische Partei Deutschlands*) in Prague and kept an underground information service going. The high quality of the information collected by the Sopade showed, however, only too conclusively that all hope of overthrowing the regime had vanished.

The KPD was, as a party dedicated to revolution, better equipped than the SPD to conduct underground opposition and felt the full force of Nazi terror immediately after the Reichstag fire. Even more than the SPD the Communists were misled by their Marxist views into expecting an inevitable collapse of the Nazi regime. They therefore allowed their most committed followers, often very courageous individuals, to attempt acts of sabotage and other activities intended to lead to Hitler's overthrow. This merely made it easier for the Gestapo to infiltrate their organisation and led to the death of many of their activists. By 1935 this kind of resistance had reached a dead end. The political parties and groupings apart from the left were even less in a position to offer any resistance. The Catholic Centre Party, once a mainstay of the Weimar Republic, voted for the Enabling Act. The former nationalist opposition of the Weimar period had allied itself with Hitler, but this did not save it from dissolution.

This left only the Churches and the Army surviving as more or less autonomous organisations within the increasingly totalitarian Nazi state. It was, in fact, in these two organisations that such organised resistance as there was in the Third Reich was mainly located. In analysing church resistance, the very different starting point of the Lutherans and the Catholics has to be considered. The Lutheran churches, organised on a regional basis, were one of the main pillars of nationalism in the Weimar period and had never come to terms with the republic. They greeted the arrival in power of Hitler with enthusiasm and events like the Day of Potsdam (see page 87) made them believe that the Third Reich was the fulfilment of their highest hopes. The Roman Catholic Church, on the other hand, had been involved in a prolonged struggle with the new German Reich in the days of Bismarck. Before 1933 the Catholic bishops had declared the National Socialist doctrine, because it was based on race, incompatible with Catholicism. In practice the antagonism between Catholicism and National Socialism had often been watered down in the years between 1930 and 1933. The Catholic Church had always been opposed to liberalism and abhorred Communism. Once Hitler was in power the German Catholic bishops retracted their former opposition to National Socialism. Under the influence of the Vice-Chancellor Papen, a Catholic, a Concordat was concluded with the Vatican in July 1933, the first time that a foreign power had entered into a treaty with the new regime. It was a great success for Hitler in his drive for respectability and acceptance. The Vatican gave up all political opposition to the regime and to the dissolution of the Centre Party. In return the Concordat seemed to give the Church freedom to run its own affairs, schools and youth organisations to a greater degree than had been the case in the Weimar period. Political conformity and surrender of its political arm, the Centre Party, seemed therefore a price worth paying, especially as Nazi Germany now constituted a mighty barrier to the spread of Bolshevism.

The Lutheran Resistance

The first major clash between Church and the Nazi state came, surprisingly, with the Lutherans and not with the Catholics. Within the Lutheran churches a faction called German Christians had obtained increasing support even before 1933. The German Christians wanted to remove all traces of Judaism from the faith and declared Jesus to be an Aryan. The Nazi authorities thought they could impose German Christianity on the Lutheran churches in return for uniting them in one Reich church. The first Reich bishop to be appointed, Müller, was a German Christian and dyed-in-the-wool Nazi. His appointment aroused opposition, as did attempts to sack 'non-Aryan' pastors. A 'Confessing Church' (*Bekennende Kirche*) was established, which in its turn declared the Nazi racist doctrines incompatible with Christianity. Many thousand Lutheran pastors supported the Confessing Church and so did many of the practising Lutheran laity. Müller and his supporters were left high and dry, and Hitler, not wishing, for the time being, to push the controversy to extremes, allowed other regional bishops, who did not support German Christianity, to remain in office. For the remaining ten years of Nazi rule the situation subsided into a kind of trench warfare. Pastors with a strong commitment to the Confessing Church ended up in concentration camps, including Martin Niemöller, a much decorated submarine commander from the First World War, who had initially been sympathetic to the Nazi take-over. Others, like Dietrich Bonhoeffer, were prevented from preaching. But Hitler, not wishing to push the many Germans who were still practising Lutherans but also loyal to the Nazi state into an impossible situation, stopped short of imposing full ideological *Gleichschaltung*. This is what men like Himmler, Alfred Rosenberg, the most prominent Nazi neo-heathen, and Martin Bormann, the increasingly influential party secretary, wanted. Hitler undoubtedly agreed with them and would have given them full reign after a final Nazi victory. (See Document, Hitler's *Table Talk*, page 50.)

The Roman Catholic Resistance

In the meantime the Catholics quickly found their hopes of the Concordat disappointed and were also pushed into growing confrontation with the regime. The work of Catholic schools and youth organisations became, in spite of the Concordat, increasingly difficult. The Nazi authorities embarked, from 1935, on a systematic campaign to discredit the Roman Catholic Church and its institutions. Special Gestapo squads entered monasteries and unearthed 'evidence' against priests, monks and nuns, leading to public trials for fraud, currency and sexual offences. Attempts were made to remove the cross from schools and this led to widespread protests among the population, so that local Nazi bosses had often to back-track. By 1937 relations between the Catholic Church and the Third Reich had become so bad that Pope Pius XI issued an encyclical 'With burning sorrow' (*Mit brennender Sorge*) about the situation in Germany. The Nazi authorities prevented it from being read from pulpits. The limited success the Catholic Church had in stopping the euthanasia campaign in 1941 (see page 101) shows that the regime wanted to postpone an all-out confrontation with the Church until after final victory. The tragedy of the resistance of the churches to the Nazi regime was that it was confined to relatively narrow issues. The Nazi racial doctrines were condemned in general and the persecution or elimination of 'non-Aryan' priests or pastors was actively resisted, but, apart from individuals, the churches, to their discredit, did not speak out against the massive crimes of the regime, such as the murder of Jews. On the other hand the churches preserved a space which the totalitarian claims of National Socialism found difficult to penetrate. They forced Hitler to postpone the full application of his ideology until after a final victory, which never came.

The Army Plot and the National-Conservative Opposition

As Hitler's rule became consolidated and even widely popular, there was only one organisation left that could oppose him effectively, the Army. Its acquiescence in the Nazi take-over and its complicity in the Night of the Long Knives were, as we have seen, crucial points in the establishment and development of the Third Reich. The senior officers of the Army were part of the national-conservative elites with whose help Hitler came to power, who shared his aim of making Germany a great power again, but who found their influence on the making of policy increasingly reduced. The Dictator was fairly and squarely in the driving seat, especially in foreign policy, and some of the generals, having to deal with the consequences of his decisions, became fearful of the risks he was taking. The potential of the Army to resist Hitler was increasingly limited by its huge expansion. The inner group of senior generals, mostly drawn from the Prussian aristocracy, were isolated in an officer corps made up of many more recently risen men who were committed Nazis. Even many of the original core group felt bound by the oath taken to Hitler, did not see how they could oppose a man who had the support of the people, and were corrupted by the opportunities and marshal's batons now showered upon them. There were others, disgusted by the moral evil of a system in which they had become trapped, who were prepared to resist regardless of Hitler's successes. It was not until 1938 that the military plot against Hitler thickened and we must turn to the evolution of his foreign policy to explain the reasons.

Resistance to the Regime

- The churches created a space into which the totalitarian claims of the Nazi state could not penetrate.

- The resistance of the churches was either concerned with general ideas, mainly the racial doctrines of the Nazis, or focused on particular cases arising out of them, for example the exclusion of non-Aryan pastors. There was no general opposition to the regime from the churches.
- The Army was the only organisation with the physical capability of overthrowing Hitler.
- The Army plots never came to fruition before 1944, because the officer corps was increasingly nazified, the senior officers surviving from the pre-Nazi era were prevented from acting by Hitler's successes and popularity, by their oath to him and by the promotions they received from him.
- A few officers retained their moral objections to the regime and were part of a wider network of a mainly national-conservative opposition. This network made contact with other opponents, from the former left-wing parties, trade unions and the churches, when the regime was clearly heading for defeat after 1942.

Questions to Consider

- In which respects was Hitler's Germany totalitarian?
- What was the 'Hitler myth' and why was it important?
- What was the system of terror in Nazi Germany?
- Why were the Jews persecuted and why was the pace of persecution uneven?
- Which groups were more able to resist Nazi power after 1933 and why was resistance not more successful?

EXAMINATION QUESTIONS

1 Why was there so little public opposition to Hitler's regime between 1933 and 1941?

2 'An ideological fanatic with no clear plan of action.' How far does the social policy of Nazi Germany support this description of Hitler?

9 Foreign Policy and War, 1933-1941

The Destruction of the Versailles System

Hitler had to move cautiously in his foreign policy when he came to power (see page 95). Every gesture foreshadowing his future aggressions, like leaving the League of Nations in October 1933, was accompanied by profuse expressions of his peaceful intentions and much was left in the hands of the traditional diplomats. Among the early initiatives that marked a clear break with previous policies the most surprising was a non-aggression pact concluded with Poland in January 1934. Throughout the Weimar years Poland had been seen as Germany's chief potential adversary. For this reason it was an article of faith, particularly in the German Army, that good relations with Russia should be cultivated, in spite of the ideological hostility to the Bolshevik regime. For a while Hitler continued this policy, but the virulent anti-Bolshevism of his propaganda and the destruction of the German Communists made it increasingly difficult. By May 1933 the secret collaboration between the Reichswehr and the Red Army was discontinued. In Warsaw the authoritarian Pilsudski regime, also strongly anti-Russian, had become disillusioned with the French alliance as the basis of Polish security.

By concluding the pact with Poland Hitler secured a number of benefits. He profiled himself strongly as Europe's bulwark against Bolshevism, something that made his regime increasingly acceptable to many people in the Western democracies. He weakened the French network of alliances in Eastern Europe and thereby put another nail in the coffin of the Versailles system. The Polish pact notwithstanding, Hitler's Germany remained dangerously isolated and widely suspect in 1934. In June 1934 Hitler paid his first official foreign visit, to Mussolini in Venice. He was thoroughly upstaged by his fellow Fascist dictator and could not hope for any favours from him. When five weeks later the Austrian Nazis mounted a coup to seize power in Vienna, during which the Austrian chancellor Dollfuss was murdered, Mussolini made it clear that he would not tolerate an infringement of Austrian independence. Hitler had to backpedal frantically by pretending that the German Government had had nothing to do with the Nazi uprising in Vienna. Hitler's first attempt to take over Austria, the *Anschluss* (juncture), had failed ignominiously.

The year 1935 opened much more auspiciously for him. In January, under the terms of the Versailles treaty, a plebiscite was held in the Saar, the coal-steel basin on Germany's western frontier, to decide whether the population wished to rejoin to Germany. Ninety-one per cent voted in favour. It was a great triumph for Hitler. The miners and steelworkers of the Saar, for long supporters of the left-wing parties, were prepared to trade their freedom for life under the Nazis. In March Hitler mounted the first of his weekend coups, in which he openly and unilaterally broke the Versailles Treaty. He reintroduced conscription, thus breaking the limitation on the size of the German army, which was the most important of the disarmament provisions imposed by the treaty on Germany. The Army was to be quickly expanded to 36 divisions and 550,000 men and an air force, hitherto secret, was to be built up. This move should have evoked an immediate countermove by the major powers which were signatories of the Versailles and Locarno treaties, Britain, France and Italy. They did indeed meet at Stresa and issued protests and declarations, but there was no action. Hitler's bluff had worked. The effect on his prestige among his own people can hardly be exaggerated.

The Beginnings of Appeasement

The so-called Stresa front soon disintegrated. Britain concluded a naval agreement with Germany, in June 1935, which fixed the strength of their respective surface fleets in the proportion 35 to 100, and of their submarine fleets at 45 to 100. It was again a major success for Hitler and appeared to go a long way towards the British alliance, which he had already advocated in *Mein Kampf.* It would cover his back while he embarked upon the acquisition of living space in Eastern Europe. This was, however, not what the British had in mind. They wanted to shore up the peace in Europe by allowing adjustments to the Versailles system. Throughout the next few years Britain was never prepared to grant Hitler a free hand in Eastern Europe. It would have produced the dominance of the Continent by one power, Germany, something Britain had fought against for centuries. In return Hitler's pledges to respect the British Empire were worth very little. In the days of air power, any country controlling the whole of Europe would threaten the very existence of Britain as an independent nation. However, successive British Governments were prepared to go a long way on the road to appeasement, not yet a word with wholly negative overtones. They were prepared to negotiate about navies, colonies, territorial adjustments in Europe, provided it was done peacefully. The last thing the British public was prepared to contemplate was another war. Britain, facing social and economic problems at home, simply did not have the resources to act as a policeman all over the world. As for France, the public was equally unprepared to face another war, and her days as the major military power in Europe were clearly numbered. The Franco-Soviet pact concluded in 1935 had limited value, for there were widespread

misgivings about an alliance with Stalin's murderous rule, which was regarded as more menacing than Hitler's by many people of right-wing views. Italy was about to break away from her Western allies altogether. Mussolini, eager to strengthen his regime by successful conquest, was about to attack Ethiopia, one of the few remaining independent countries in Africa. The Abyssinian war brought him into conflict with the League of Nations, of which the mainstays were still Britain and France. The way was prepared for a switch of alliances by Italy from the Western democracies to Germany.

The Remilitarisation of the Rhineland

In March 1936 Hitler used this favourable international situation for another weekend coup, his most risky up to date and the one with the most far-reaching consequences, the remilitarisation of the Rhineland. Although the Allies had withdrawn their troops from the Rhineland in June 1930, a demilitarised zone was left. German troops moved into this zone, but they had orders to withdraw immediately in case of a French countermove. Although this was a life-and-death matter for France, as subsequent events were to prove, the French Government was unable to act. France was deeply divided and in the midst of an election campaign that was to bring to a power a Popular Front Government, an alliance of Socialists and Communists, under the Socialist Léon Blum. The right wing in France felt that Blum was almost worse than Hitler and were unhappy about the Franco-Soviet pact. The French consulted the British, but London was unwilling to move when British interests were not directly threatened. Hitler's propaganda and peace offering which accompanied his coup were taken seriously and it was said that the Germans were only moving into their back garden.

The remilitarisation of the Rhineland changed the equation of power in Europe at a stroke. France's alliances in Eastern Europe became worthless, because the French army could no longer come to the assistance of countries like Poland or Czechoslovakia without a major war. Small countries all over Europe hastened to make their peace with Germany. The last occasion when Hitler could have been stopped without war had been missed. In Germany belief in Hitler as a miracle worker was becoming deeply entrenched among the masses. Grumbles about the regime, the struggle with the churches, the economic shortages were forgotten. At the top the diplomats and generals who had expressed doubts about Hitler's gamble were silenced. It was becoming virtually impossible for anyone to resist a man who was always being proved right by events and who had more popular support than anybody in previous German history. Most dangerous of all, Hitler began to believe in his own myth. It was after the Rhineland occupation that he said 'I go along the path to which Providence has called me with the assurance of a sleepwalker'.

Document. From Hitler's secret Four-Year Plan memorandum, August 1936
Politics are the conduct and the course of the historical struggle of nations for life ... Germany will as always have to be regarded as the focus of the Western world against the attacks of Bolshevism ... if we do not succeed in bringing the German Army as rapidly as possible to the rank of premier army of the world so far as its training, raising of units, armaments and, above all, its spiritual education also is concerned, then Germany will be lost!

Economic Preparation for War

No matter how sensational Hitler's triumphs, they could not alter the fact that Germany did not really have the resources for the wars of conquest and domination the Führer was heading for. Armaments had accounted for 1.6 per cent of the social product in 1933 and this had risen to 13.75 by 1936. It was not a sustainable situation. Schacht, still the most influential figure in the management of the German economy had, up to this point, been able to contain the pressures that were building up within the German productive system. Wages were tightly controlled, as we have seen, and there was also reasonably effective price control. Excessive purchasing power was syphoned off through various schemes of compulsory saving, such as that mentioned in connection with the Volkswagen. Very tight control of foreign currency had been introduced at an early stage. Barter agreements with countries in the Balkans and in Latin America helped with the supply of raw materials. Nevertheless, serious shortages constantly threatened both production and consumer supplies. Schacht did not think that Germany could be decoupled from the world economy. This meant that there had to be a limit to rearmament and that further changes in Germany's international position had to be sought by agreement with the major powers, in particular with Britain. Schacht began to lose his influence in 1936, but he was still taken sufficiently seriously in Paris and London in 1937 to make the British and French Governments think that there could be some kind of economic appeasement of Germany. In return for handing back some former German colonies, and other concessions, Germany would confine herself to peaceful adjustments in Europe.

All this was of no interest to Hitler. In a secret memorandum of August 1936 the dictator insisted on the absolute priority of rearmament, for only in this way could the central problem of the German nation's existence be solved and living space be acquired. The German Armed Forces had to be ready for war within four years. Everything had to be unconditionally subordinated to this supreme national necessity and politics must come before economics. The arguments were very reminiscent of the pages of *Mein Kampf* and they set the framework for future developments. It was a circular argument: rearmament for war was an absolute necessity, but such a policy left no option but war.

- Historians have raised the question to what extent Hitler's course of territorial expansion after the end of 1937 was driven by economic pressures, but these pressures were of Hitler's own making and were themselves the product of his intention to seek expansion by conquest.
- Göring was put in charge of a Four-Year Plan to make Germany self-sufficient. Under him a whole new bureaucracy was created to force the rapid production of substitute materials, such as synthetic fuel and artificial rubber. German industry was subjected to an unprecedented degree of state control, but the new bureaucracy was itself largely recruited from some of Germany's industrial giants, such as the chemical combine I.G. Farben.
- The German economy moved another large step away from the market economy. As for the consumer, Hitler was anxious that he should not be put under too much pressure. Always at the back of his mind was his fear of another 1918, when, as he saw it, economic hardship had forced Germany into revolution and defeat.
- By 1937 unemployment had disappeared and particularly in industries connected with rearmament there was a shortage of labour. Incomes rose, but there was both a dearth of goods on which to spend them and a decline in the quality of goods. Clothing was no longer made of wool or silk, but of coarse artificial fibres. Instead of butter there was margarine.
- To earn the wages with which he was then unable to buy very much the German worker had to work long hours. Even if statistically the standard of living in 1938 had scarcely caught up with that of 1928, the German man in the street compared his situation not with the 1920s but with the dire conditions experienced in the Great Depression and he credited the regime and, above all, Hitler with the improvement. (See Table 9)
- Nevertheless, the German economy, overtaxed by Hitler's rapid drive for rearmament, was on a tightrope in 1937. It would sooner, rather than later, have lurched into a crisis if Hitler had not changed the whole framework by headlong territorial expansion.

The Blitzkrieg Strategy

There remained problems and dilemmas which no amount of political will and sensational foreign policy successes could resolve. Because of the fundamental inadequacy of German resources the rearmament programme had breadth rather than depth. A number of weapons which in the then current state of technology were essential for offensive warfare, such as tanks and attack bombers, were produced in considerable quantities, but the reserves of all kinds of war materials necessary for a more prolonged campaign were inadequate. This dictated a strategy which became known as *Blitzkrieg*, lightning war. Germany would have to widen her resource base by a series of lightning strikes against weaker opponents before risking a general war between the great powers. In Hitler's view the optimum time for a general war for Germany would be the early 1940s, when her rearmament would have proceeded sufficiently far while that of her potential opponents would not yet have caught up. There were therefore military, as well as political and psychological reasons, why Hitler became obsessed with the need to force the pace.

Table 9: Industrial output, consumption of goods, earnings and cost of living

	Total industrial production	*Consumption of goods*	*Real earnings per hour*	*Real earnings per week*	*Cost of living*
	(1928 = 100)		*(1936 = 100)*		
1928	100	100	100.9	102.2	121.8
1929	100	97	104.7	103.6	123.7
1930	87	91	105.7	99.2	119.0
1931	70	82	106.4	95.1	109.3
1932	58	74	100.7	88.5	96.6
1933	66	80	99.8	92.5	94.8
1934	83	93	99.7	96.7	97.3
1935	96	91	99.6	97.6	98.8
1936	107	98	100.0	100.0	100.0
1937	117	103	101.6	103.0	100.5
1938	125	108	104.7	107.5	100.9
1939	132	108	107.2	111.1	101.4
1940	128	102	106.4	111.0	104.5
1941	131	104	109.2	115.5	107.0
1942	132	93	108.6	113.3	109.7
1943	149	98	107.0	112.2	111.2
1944	146	93	104.7	108.6	113.6

Contradictions in the Nazi Ideology

A number of other dilemmas arose as a result of Hitler's determination to mobilise for war with the utmost rapidity. The labour shortage required the return of women to work, when the Nazi ideology had at first led to their withdrawal from the labour market (see page 89). The number of women in employment rose by 1.3 million between 1933 and 1939. Only in the higher professional sphere was the reduction in female employment desired by Nazi ideology adhered to. As it was, women were not as fully mobilised during the war in Germany as they were in Britain, largely because Hitler thought it might be damaging to morale. By then there was enough forced labour from the occupied countries to make the need for female labour less urgent. Another Nazi ideological aim, the boosting of the farming population, was also sidetracked by the need to increase industrial production for war. The 'blood and soil' aspect of Nazism had led to a number of enactments, including one which tied smaller farms to the families traditionally holding them (*Erbhofsgesetz*, Law for Hereditary Farmsteads), so that they could no longer be sold freely. But now there was pressure to maximise agricultural production and small family farms were not the best way to obtain it. There was again a drift into the cities and industrial employment. A reduced rural workforce had to work ever harder. In the role allotted to farmers and women, the fear of the modern world and the wish to return to an allegedly more wholesome past, which was so important an aspect of National Socialism, was uppermost. But if the aim of conquest, which was also central to Nazism, was to be realised, the most modern methods and technologies had to be used.

Territorial Expansion Begins

The remilitarisation of the Rhineland was only the most important of the developments in 1936 and 1937 that were creating a situation increasingly favourable to Hitler's plans of expansion. After the completion of the conquest of Ethiopia Mussolini was gradually turning to Germany as an ally. In November 1936 he coined the term 'axis' to describe the relationship between Rome and Berlin. In September 1937 he paid a state visit to Germany, during which Hitler pulled out all the stops to impress his fellow-dictator with the power and purpose of the Third Reich. Austria was therefore left isolated and in July 1936 had had to sign a treaty which moved her decidedly into the German sphere of influence. Hitler intervened on the spur of the moment in the Spanish Civil War, which had broken out in 1936, and thereby acquired another eventual ally in Franco, a testing ground for some of his weapons and a useful source of raw materials. In May 1937 Neville Chamberlain had become British Prime Minister, committed to pursue an active policy of appeasement in Europe. He hoped that deals could be struck with Germany and Italy that would satisfy their reasonable aspirations and thus create greater stability in Europe.

The Hossbach Memorandum

On 5 November 1937 Hitler had a secret meeting with his leading military men, Blomberg, the Minister of Defence, the commanders of the Army, Navy and Air Force, Fritsch, Raeder and Göring, and his foreign minister von Neurath. The original purpose of the meeting was to get Hitler to decide on the allocation of scarce steel between Army and Navy, but this was just the sort of problem he did not wish to get drawn into. He therefore harangued his listeners for three hours about his future plans. Notes were taken by his military adjutant, Colonel Hossbach, and subsequently reproduced in a memorandum. The Hossbach Memorandum was used by the prosecution in the Nuremberg War Crimes Trial after the war to substantiate the charge that aggressive war was being planned.

Document. From the Hossbach Memorandum, minutes of the conference in the Reich Chancellery, 5 November 1937.

Present: Hitler, Blomberg (Defence Minister), Fritsch (C in C Army), Raeder (C in C Navy), Göring (C in C Air Force), Neurath (Foreign Minister), Colonel Hossbach (Military Adjutant).

The Führer began by stating that the subject of the present conference was of such importance that its discussion would, in other countries, be a matter for a full Cabinet meeting ... he asked ... that his exposition be regarded, in the event of his death, as his last will and testament.

The aim of German policy was to make secure and to preserve the racial mass [*Volksmasse*] and to enlarge it ...

The question for Germany was: where could she achieve the greatest gain at the lowest cost? German policy had to reckon with two hate-filled antagonists, Britain and France, to whom a German colossus in the centre of Europe was a thorn in the flesh, and both countries were opposed to any further strengthening of Germany's position either in Europe or overseas power politics ... France's position was more favourable than that of Britain ... but France was going to be confronted with internal difficulties ...

Contingency 1 (period 1943-45): After this date only a change for the worse, from our point of view, could be expected ... Our relative strength would decrease in relation to the rearmament that would by then have been carried out by the rest of the world ... If the Führer was still living it was his unalterable determination to solve Germany's problem of space by 1943-45 at the latest. The necessity for action before 1943-45 would arise in contingencies 2 and 3.

Contingency 2: If internal strife in France should develop into such a domestic crisis as to absorb the French army completely and render it incapable of use for war against Germany, then the time for action against the Czechs would have come.

Contingency 3: If France should be so embroiled in war with another state that she could not 'proceed' against Germany. For the improvement of our politico-military position, our first objective, in the event of being embroiled in war, must be to overthrow Czechoslovakia and Austria simultaneously in order to remove the threat to our flank in any possible operation against the West ... Actually, the Führer believed that almost certainly Britain, and probably France as well, had already tacitly written off the Czechs and were reconciled to the fact that this question would be cleared up in due course by Germany.

While such a document does not entirely support the hard and fast interpretation put on it in a court of law, it does show the way Hitler's mind was running at this time. He expected that in 1938 opportunities would occur for territorial acquisition, in particular in respect of Czechoslovakia. He thought that France and Britain would not be able or willing to intervene to help the Czechs. He repeated the old arguments about the need for living space already used in *Mein Kampf*. Although the memorandum records their words only very briefly, it is clear that Blomberg and Fritsch, possibly also Neurath, were somewhat alarmed by the Führer's remarks.

It is therefore hardly surprising that when, a few weeks later, an opportunity occurred to get rid of all three of them, Hitler pounced. Blomberg had married his secretary, who had a record as a prostitute; Fritsch was falsely accused of homosexuality. Some of the evidence was manufactured by Göring and Himmler. Simultaneously, a large number of generals and senior diplomats were retired and Ribbentrop succeeded Neurath as foreign minister. Hitler personally assumed command of the Armed Forces *(Oberkommando der Wehrmacht,* OKW). It was a crisis of the regime not unlike the Night of the Long Knives in 1934, although this time there was no bloodshed. Again Hitler was the undisputed winner and the national-conservative elites, who had helped him into the saddle, suffered a further loss of influence.

The Austrian Anschluss

The Führer was determined to overcome any feeling in foreign capitals that there was a crisis inside Germany by vigorous action. Events in Austria had just played a card into his hands. The Austrian Government, headed since 1934 by Chancellor Schuschnigg, was desperate to maintain itself against the constant threats of the Austrian Nazis, encouraged by the treaty of 1936. A search of a Nazi office in Vienna in January 1938 revealed preparations for a coup similar to that which had occurred in 1934. Hitler used this as an excuse to summon Schuschnigg to the Berghof, where he threatened him severely. It was a way of dealing with the head of a sovereign government hitherto unknown. On 9 March 1938, Schuschnigg, with virtually no cards left, announced a plebiscite, in which the Austrian

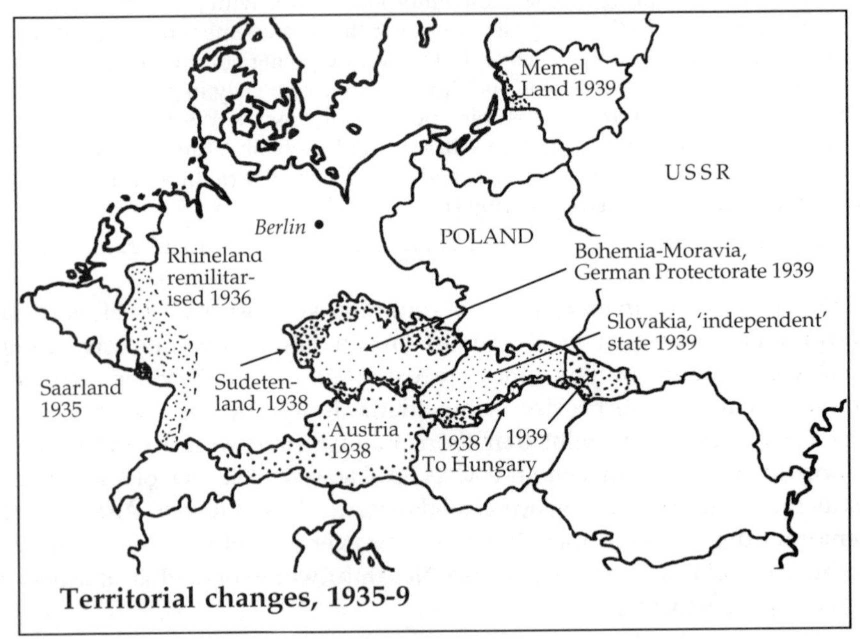

Territorial changes, 1935-9

people were asked to affirm the continuing independence of their country. Hitler was now forced into immediate action. He assured himself of Mussolini's non-intervention. Göring in a series of telephone calls to Vienna forced the resignation of Schuschnigg, his replacement by a Nazi, Seyss-Inquart, who was then instructed to invite German troops into his country. Hitler himself entered Austria on 13 March in the wake of his troops. When he experienced the enthusiasm with which the Austrians welcomed him he decided to annex Austria as another 'Land of the Reich'. He entered Vienna in triumph. In the eyes of the German people his elevation into a god-like figure reached new heights. Without firing a shot he seemed to have achieved what even Bismarck had failed to accomplish, the unification of all the German countries. The very extent of his triumphs seemed to put Hitler under a compulsion to trump them with ever greater ones. He had, as we have seen, put all his cards, not on some stabilisation or consolidation, if that had ever been a possibility given the all-embracing nature of his revolutionary aims, but on overcoming all contradictions by moving forward at ever greater speed. It was as if the difficulties and depressions which afflict all societies at one time or another could only be mastered by unleashing ever more frantic dynamism and achieving ever greater triumphs.

The Czech Crisis and the Munich Agreement

The Austrian Anschluss left Czechoslovakia dangerously exposed, surrounded on three sides by German territory. The Czech state, with its German minority of over three million, known as the Sudeten Germans, had been a mote in the eyes of German nationalists since its foundation in 1918. Hitler, as we have seen, was seeking an early opportunity to destroy it. Within days of returning from Vienna he gave instructions to the leader of the Sudeten Germans, Konrad Henlein, to put forward demands which the Czech Government could not possibly accept. By May the next great crisis that would bring Europe to the brink of war was in full swing. Benes, the Czech President, to demonstrate that his country would not submit without a fight, mobilised his forces. France, tied by treaty obligations to come to the aid of the Czechs, had to show her hand and even Britain, in spite of Chamberlain's determined pursuit of appeasement, had to declare her readiness to stand by France in case of war. Hitler temporarily held his hand, but now gave definite instructions to his armed forces to prepare to smash Czecholovakia by military action in the near future.

Germany and Britain, Hitler and Chamberlain, now became the principal antagonists. Chamberlain left no stone unturned to resolve the crisis peacefully. He envisaged a cession of the Sudenten areas by the Czechs, but the preservation of a rump Czechoslovakia. In the pursuit of this objective the Czechs tended to be seen by the British Government not as potential victims, but increasingly as the obstacle to a peaceful resolution of the crisis. Chamberlain's policy, given the world-wide preoccupations of Britain and the intense reluctance of the public to risk war, had a certain rationality, but unfortunately the British Prime Minister faced an antagonist who was not rational and wanted war. When the crisis reached its climax in September 1938 Chamberlain flew three times to see Hitler to persuade him to accept a peaceful settlement.

In the meantime Hitler's high-risk gamble had aroused opposition at the highest level in the German Army and among German diplomats. Most of those who now began to have doubts about Hitler and his methods were typical members of the national-conservative elites, who had for so long done his bidding and shared many of his objectives, but they saw that his unrestrained drive towards war was risking the very existence of Germany. The German opposition made contact with the British Government and tried to persuade it to adopt a firm line against Hitler, which would then lead them to depose him. The British had little confidence in these undertakings and it was indeed a fatal weakness of the German opposition that they made their moves against Hitler dependent on support from the outside. We will never know whether a coup against Hitler would really have materialised, for the convening of a four-power conference at Munich on 29 September put an end to the plans of the conspirators. At this conference the cession of the Sudeten German areas to Germany was agreed and imposed upon the Czechs. It was Hitler's second great triumph in 1938. He had incorporated into what was now called the Greater German Reich over ten million German speakers in Austria and the Sudetenland without firing a shot. He himself was, however, dissatisfied. Chamberlain had baulked him of his aim of smashing Czechoslovakia by war. It was clearly demonstrated that in Germany people were afraid of war and immensely relieved when it was averted. At the end of his life, seven years later, Hitler still thought things would have gone better for him if war had broken out in 1938.

The March into Prague

The sense of relief produced by the Munich agreement was short-lived. In Britain the opponents of appeasement, among whom Winston Churchill was the most prominent, declared it to be a shameful surrender. The anti-Jewish pogrom of November 1938 (see page 105) shocked public opinion in all Western countries and highlighted the barbaric nature of Hitler's rule. On the very day following the Night of Crystal the Führer told German newspaper editors that from henceforth the German people would have to be psychologically prepared for war and that his talk of peace in the previous few years had only been a tactical necessity. On 15 March 1939, less than six months after Munich, German troops marched into Prague, the Czech capital, in what proved to be the last of Hitler's major bloodless conquests. On this occasion he scarcely bothered to provide any justification for his move and the German propaganda screen was patently thin. His solemn declarations that he was only interested in uniting all Germans in one Reich were obviously untrue and so was his statement that the Sudetenland was his last territorial claim in Europe.

With hindsight, one can see that Hitler was now overreaching himself. He had administered a fatal blow to Chamberlain's policy of appeasement. The British Prime Minister was still eager to save something from the wreckage, but his room for manoeuvre was now narrowly circumscribed. British public and parliamentary opinion was convinced that deals with Hitler were no longer possible and Chamberlain's own foreign secretary, Lord Halifax, shared that conviction. The British Government tried frantically to erect 'Halt - Major Road Ahead' signs, as Halifax put it, in Hitler's path by giving guarantees of assistance to Poland and Rumania. Poland was clearly marked out as Germany's next victim. Having participated in the dismemberment of Czechoslovakia at Munich the luckless Poles now found themselves in a pincer embrace very similar to that which had closed on the Czechs after the Austrian Anschluss. From internal documents now available to us it is clear that the Führer was not deterred by the British guarantee to Poland. Already at the meeting recorded by Colonel Hossbach in November 1937 he had referred to Britain and France as 'hate-filled enemies'. He no longer hoped for a British alliance, but believed that Britain would not go to war for the countries of Eastern Europe. So far this belief had proved correct. At a meeting with his service chiefs on 23 May 1939 he continued to proclaim this belief and assured his listeners that the war with Poland, for which he had initiated preparations, would be fought against that country in isolation. But he also said that if Britain and France were drawn into such a war he was quite ready to fight it.

The Nazi-Soviet Pact

As Europe was heading for war in the summer of 1939 the crucial diplomatic question was which side the Soviet Union would support. On the face of it the ideological enmity to the death between National Socialism and Communism seemed to suggest an obvious answer. The ideological hostility had been enshrined in treaty form in the Anti-Comintern Pact betweeen Germany and Japan in November 1936, to which Italy adhered a year later. Russia was thus surrounded by a hostile triangle. Japan's own separate campaign to spread her power in the Far East throughout the 1930s had, in fact, been yet another constellation favouring Hitler, for it created great problems for the British Empire and in due course for the United States. Stalin and his foreign minister, Litvinov, had since 1935 made a series of moves to construct a common front with the Western democracies against Hitler and had concluded a pact with France (see pages 111-112). As we have seen, suspicion of the Bolshevik regime not unnaturally ran deep in the democratic countries. To this was added the horror provoked by Stalin's brutal treatment of the peasants in the Ukraine and his devastating purges. The purges also led Western military leaders to put a low value on Russia's military power. A country which had got rid of 80 per cent of its senior military officers on account of their alleged unreliability could hardly be taken seriously. The underestimation of Russia's military capacity was paralleled by an overestimation of Poland. Russia was excluded from the Munich conference. But the German march into Prague at last convinced the British and French governments that a military alliance with Russia was necessary to give substance to the deterrence of Hitler. Negotiations started, but there were great obstacles, the most serious being the fact that the countries whom it was intended to help, Poland and Rumania, refused to have Soviet troops on their soil. In the light of what happened to them after 1945 this refusal was understandable.

Stalin gradually became convinced that the Western powers were out to deflect the full fury of German military might eastwards and that he would be pulling their chestnuts out of the fire if he concluded a military pact with them. In May 1939 he dropped his Jewish foreign minister, Litvinov, closely connected with the policy of collective security through the League of Nations, and appointed Molotov, an immediate associate, in his place. On the German side Ribbentrop convinced Hitler that an effective anti-British front required at least a tactical agreement with Russia. When everyone knew in August 1939 that a German attack on Poland was imminent and while French and British negotiators were still in Moscow, the Russians suddenly accepted a visit from Ribbentrop. On 23 August 1939 the Nazi-Soviet Non-Aggression Pact was made public. In a secret annex the two countries agreed on a demarcation line in Poland that would hand a band about two hundred miles wide over to Russia. The Baltic states and Finland were also declared to be in the Russian sphere of interest. It was one of the most infamous deals in history. Only two totalitarian regimes could have concluded it, for only weeks before they had painted each other in the blackest of colours in their propaganda. As it was, both brutal dictators had reason to regret it in the longer run. Hitler handed Stalin a broad band of territory, which he had to traverse in his attack on Russia less than two years later. Stalin thought he had diverted Hitler from his patch, but by the summer of 1940, after the defeat of France, he was facing the German Army alone on the Continent, something that nearly led to the military collapse of the Soviet Union in 1941.

Immediately the Nazi-Soviet pact gave Hitler reason to expect that he could now deal with Poland in isolation and that Britain and France would be deterred from honouring their commitment to the Poles. This turned out to be an illusion and a further disappointment awaited the German Dictator. His Italian colleague, Mussolini, was not prepared to enter a general war at this stage. These disappointments made Hitler hesitate only briefly in his rush towards war. The German attack on Poland, originally scheduled for 26 August 1939, was postponed till 1 September. All last-minute efforts at mediation failed and the attack precipitated the expected declarations of war by Britain and France.

The Second World War. Hitler's Early Victories

Although Hitler had ordered a massive propaganda smoke screen to convince the German public that Polish provocation had forced him into military action there was little enthusiasm for war in Germany. Nothing like the patriotic upsurge of August 1914 occurred, but Germany's swift victory over Poland seemed, once again, to prove Hitler right. Britain and France, although they had declared war, were unwilling or unable to launch any major offensive to help the Poles. In itself the victory in Poland did not, however, solve the basic German strategic dilemma. Germany still had an inadequate resource base and the Polish campaign had shown that there were many weaknesses in her rearmament. The pact with Russia had relieved her of a two-front war and had given her access to the raw materials of the Soviet Union. This largely blunted the danger from a blockade that had proved so devastating in the First World War, but it also made Germany dependent to some extent on the Soviet Union.

Immediately after the Polish campaign Hitler pressed his generals to mount an attack in the West. They were reluctant, mindful of the stalemate of 1914-18. There was again the possibility of a military coup against Hitler, but eventually the weather prevented further moves.

In the winter of 1939/40 the Soviet Union attacked Finland, which the Nazi-Soviet pact had put into the Soviet sphere of influence. Public opinion in Britain and France wanted assistance to be offered to the Finns. If such an initiative had fully developed it might well have led to hostilities between the USSR and the Western powers, with incalculable consequences for the future course of the Second World War. Preparations were made for a British and French military expedition to Northern Norway. Before this Allied expedition could get under way Hitler pre-empted it by his own attack on Norway and Denmark, in April 1940. It was again a swift victory and eventually, by June, British forces had to be evacuated from Norway. The success of the German attack in Scandinavia led to the fall of the Chamberlain Government in Britain and on 10 May 1940 a Coalition Government under Churchill took its place. It was the day when the German offensive in the West started. Although the French army, aided by the small British Expeditionary Force, was sufficiently large and well equipped to have fought a defensive campaign successfully, it was quickly overwhelmed by the superior German strategy. Within six weeks France had to sue for an armistice.

Hitler at the Height of his Power

In Germany Hitler was now hailed as 'the greatest commander of all times', a military as well as a political genius. Many options, political and military, were open to him. A multitude of plans and blueprints were being prepared by the various agencies, governmental and party, of the Third Reich. National Socialism looked like the wave of the future, the ignominious collapse of France conclusive proof of the decadence of democracy. Events were to show, however, that the ideology of National Socialism and Hitler's own thinking could never break away from reliance on sheer brute force and domination. When the French campaign was scarcely over Hitler was already ordering plans to be made for a war against Russia.

For the moment Hitler hoped that the British would at last see reason and make peace, leaving him free to turn eastward. He ordered preparations for an invasion of the British Isles, Operation Sea Lion, to reinforce his offer of peace to Britain with a threat. It was always clear that Operation Sea Lion required the achievement of air supremacy by the Luftwaffe over the British airspace. When the RAF won the Battle of Britain in September 1940 the invasion of Britain had to be postponed. There were also other strategies that Hitler tentatively explored for putting the British under pressure. With the help of France and Spain he could mount an operation in the Western Mediterranean, against Gibraltar and into North Africa. Meetings Hitler had with Pétain, the ruler of unoccupied Vichy France, and with Franco, the Spanish dictator, in October 1940 were not productive. In the Mediterranean Hitler's freedom of manoeuvre was somewhat limited by his ally Mussolini, who had entered the war just

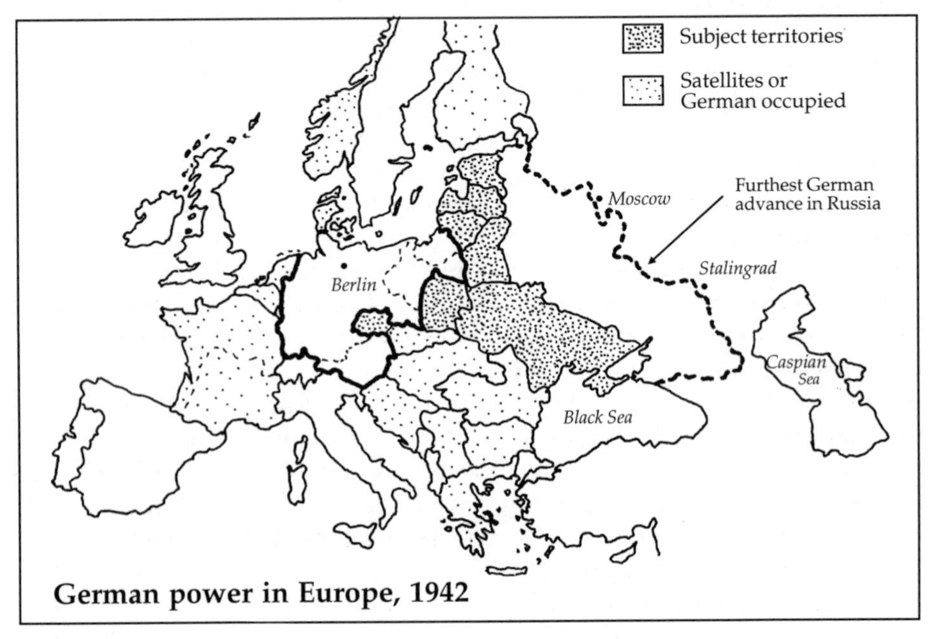

German power in Europe, 1942

before the fall of France. Hitler was further confirmed in his view that an attack on Russia was the best option when in November Molotov, the Russian Foreign Minister, paid a visit to Berlin. Demands for territorial compensation and spheres of influence in Eastern and South-Eastern Europe put forward by Molotov were not acceptable to Hitler. On 18 December 1940 he issued a directive for Operation Barbarossa: 'The German Armed Forces must be prepared to defeat the Soviet Union in a rapid campaign, even before the end of the war with England'.

It was what Hitler had always wanted and now it made considerable military sense. By defeating Russia Germany would control Europe from the Atlantic to the Urals and would be in an impregnable position. Britain's situation would become hopeless and the United States would be precluded from interfering in Europe and in a future global clash might suffer defeat. Everything pointed to a swift German victory in Russia. It had taken the Russians months to defeat the Finns, a nation of three millions. The option of trading space, as they had done in the days of Napoleon, was no longer open to them. Their forces would have to stand and fight in Western Russia in order to protect their industrial areas, without which they could not continue the fight. Hitler did not encounter significant objections from his generals to his proposed attack on Russia, as he had done so often with his previous plans. The attack, originally scheduled for 15 May, was delayed by the need of the German forces to secure their flank in the Balkans. Mussolini, eager not to be entirely overshadowed by his erstwhile disciple Hitler, had, without consulting the Germans, attacked Greece in October 1940. Italian forces got stuck a few miles beyond the Greek-Albanian border. The Germans were already planning to come to their rescue when a coup in Yugoslavia in March 1941 threatened to turn that country from a German into a British ally. In another Blitzkrieg the Wehrmacht swept into Yugoslavia and Greece and both countries capitulated.

Hitler's Blitzkrieg Fails in Russia

On 22 June 1941 the intended blitzkrieg on Russia started. Initially, German forces cut through the Russian army like a hot knife through butter and huge numbers of prisoners were taken. By mid-July the Germans thought they had won, but at the end of July the advance of their central army group was halted. Although by the beginning of October the Germans were moving forward again on all sectors in Russia, by November it began to be seen by the German leadership from Hitler down that the Russian blitzkrieg had failed. On 27 November Hitler told a visiting foreign statesman: 'If once the German nation is no longer strong enough and willing to make the sacrifice of shedding its own blood for its very existence, then it will perish and will be annihilated by another stronger power'. It was typical of his social-Darwinist thinking and he was to repeat such sentiments when in 1945 all was collapsing around him. Two days later Todt, the Nazi engineer who had built the autobahns and was, until his death in an air crash a few weeks later, the Minister responsible for munitions, told Hitler that from an armaments point of view Germany could no longer win the war.

A week later the Soviet counter offensive west of Moscow started and on 7 December the Japanese attack on Pearl Harbor brought the USA into the war in the Far East. Hitler now declared war on the Americans, thus making their intervention in the European war certain, a decision that has often been portrayed as particularly irrational. In fact, Hitler had been anxious throughout the previous weeks that the Japanese should not reach some kind of understanding with the USA that would have left the Americans free to concentrate on intervention in Europe. He regarded the US as a virtual belligerent on the side of Britain and still hoped to defeat Russia conclusively in 1942. More than ever Hitler was now staking everything on a huge gamble, unlikely to succeed. It was at this point that many people in Britain, from Churchill down, felt that a final victory for the Allies was no longer just a hope but a certainty.

The Third Reich on its Way to Destruction

A war that had started through Hitler's determination to smash Poland had become a worldwide conflagration of unprecedented ferocity and destructiveness. The gamble that Germany could widen her resource base and produce a progressively more favourable constellation had, but for Britain's stubborn refusal to make peace, been remarkably successful, but it had now failed. In the first two years of the war Germany's easy military triumphs were achieved at relatively low human and material cost. Hitler's reluctance to impose too many sacrifices on the home front had continued without serious consequences. The mobilisation that had got under way in the middle 1930s went on at full pace and measures to husband scarce resources, such as food rationing for the ordinary consumer, were introduced. More men had to join the armed forces, but there was not at this stage, and not even later in the war, anything like the mobilisation of women that took place in Britain. From 1940 increasing resources, commodities as well as labour, became available from the occupied countries, so that the German consumer did not experience too many shortages. It was only from 1942, organised by Albert Speer, that German war production really got into its stride and, in spite of the Allied bombing, it reached its peak in the summer of 1944. More than seven million foreign labourers, forced to work in Germany, many of them never to return, made this possible. Over three million Russian prisoners of war died, a holocaust almost comparable to that inflicted on the Jews.

The real radicalisation of the regime, both politically and economically, began with the war in Russia and even more so with its failure as a blitzkrieg in the winter of 1941/42. Hitler had made it clear to his

Document. From Hitler's *Table Talk*, 27 July 1941
It should be possible for us to control this region to the East with two hundred and fifty thousand men plus a cadre of good administrators. Let's learn from the English, who with two hundred and fifty thousand men in all, including fifty thousand soldiers, govern four hundred million Indians. This space in Russia must always be dominated by Germans. Nothing would be a worse mistake on our part than to seek to educate the masses there. It is to our interest that the people should know just enough to recognise the signs on the roads ... We'll take the southern part of the Ukraine, especially the Crimea, and make it an exclusively German colony. There will be no harm in pushing out the population that's there now ...

---

commanders that this was to be an ideological war of annihilation, different in kind to previous wars. All traces of Bolshevism were to be eradicated and the Russians as a people, deprived of all their skills, reduced to a slave people, servicing the German settlers to be introduced into the Russian space. An order of the Führer of 6 June 1941, which has become known as the Commissar Order, decreed the immediate shooting on sight of all 'political commissars', a category which could in practice prove very wide and gave discretion for the indiscriminate murder of partisans, Jews and others. Whereas in Poland the implementation of genocide was mainly the work of Heydrich's *Einsatzgruppen*, in Russia the Army itself was implicated. The brutality meted out to the Russian civilian population by the invaders was entirely counterproductive. Initially, there were signs that the German troops were welcome in some areas, for example in the Ukraine, where Stalin had been responsible for the mass killings of peasants. This mood changed quickly under the impact of Nazi atrocities. Resistance stiffened and behind the German lines partisan warfare flared up.

In the summer of 1941, when Nazi expectations of a final victory were at their highest, the process was also set in motion to accomplish 'the final solution of the Jewish question in the German area of influence in Europe'. This was the phrase used, avoiding the word 'murder', in a letter from Göring to Heydrich, dated 31 July 1941, asking the latter to make the necessary organisational arrangements. There may have been an initial intention to push all European Jews beyond the Urals, in the course of which forced migration many of them would perish anyway. When the Russian campaign was halted before Moscow, this was no longer an option and it was at this point that the death camps equipped with gas chambers, notably Auschwitz, began to operate, based on the experience of killing people in the euthanasia campaign (see pages 101-102).

The holocaust ranks as a crime unique in history, because modern bureaucratic methods were used to annihilate whole categories of people in death factories, in which even such remains as the gold in the teeth of the victims was subsequently exploited. Although it was a secret operation,

Document. Letter from Himmler to the Chief of the Reich Security Office, 8 September 1943

Concerning the question of sexual relations with labourers from the Baltic states:

1. I am in favour of lifting the prohibiton on sexual intercourse for Estonians and Latvians and with Estonians and Latvians.
2. I wish the prohibiton to be maintained for all Lithuanians male and female. The Lithuanians are a people whose behaviour and racial value is so low that a lifting of the prohibiton is not justified.

---

there was a general awareness in Germany that great atrocities were being committed in the East. Through crimes like the holocaust Hitler cut off all possibility of retreat for himself and his followers and made the German people his accomplices, depriving them of any escape from their increasingly dire situation.

Gradually the spell that Hitler had cast upon the German people began to weaken under the impact of defeat, especially after the surrender of a whole German army at Stalingrad in January 1943. The Führer was hardly seen or heard by the German public after 1942. He never visited any of the bombed German cities to boost morale and shut himself up in his headquarters in the dark forests of East Prussia. The role of terror and of the SS in maintaining the regime increased, for in war-time the slightest sign of disaffection, such as listening to foreign radio stations, was punishable by death. There was, however, no mass resistance, for political alternatives to Nazism no longer existed. The plot by army officers against Hitler, which eventually led to the failed attempt to kill him on 20 July 1944, had wide ramifications, but no mass support. All the evidence indicates that when Hitler survived the assassination attempt there was still a sense of relief among ordinary Germans. Many found it hard to believe that he did not still have some trick up his sleeve, perhaps the secret weapons claimed by his propaganda. The seduction of the German nation by National Socialism and Hitler only ended for good with the suicide of the Führer in his Berlin bunker on 30 April 1945. By this time the modern German nation state founded by Bismarck some eighty years before had ceased to exist.

Questions to Consider

- Why was the remilitarisation of the Rhineland, 1936, so important to Hitler and Germany's power in Europe?
- How well prepared, politically and economically, was Germany for war by 1939?

EXAMINATION QUESTIONS

1. 'Hitler's major foreign policy objective after 1933 was to prepare Germany for a racial war against the Soviet Union.' Discuss.
2. How much did Germany owe its failure in the Second World War to Hitler?

10 The Historiography of German History

The Nationalist School of Historians

In a country with so chequered a past as Germany the writing of history easily becomes a tool used by successive regimes to legitimise their existence. Until 1945 the generally accepted view of German history was that the nation state established in 1870 was the natural culmination of German history. Historians played a notable part in creating the nationalism which made the unification of the many separate states in the German-speaking area possible. They argued that German rulers in the Middle Ages had wasted their strength in pursuing aims universal to the whole of Christendom, while neglecting the unity of their German home base. In the meantime modern nation states were gradually emerging in Britain and France. Germany missed out on this development and became divided into innumerable small units, the object rather than the subject of history. Therefore, she had a lot of catching up to do in the nineteenth century. A whole school of historians extolled the mission of Prussia as the German state destined to bring about the modern revival of the German Reich. In this historical view the state had to be strong, both internally and externally, to safeguard German unity against its many potential enemies at home and abroad and the primacy of foreign policy (see page 7) was therefore taken for granted.

This approach to German history was almost universal in the German historical profession until 1945 and only a few outsiders challenged it. If anything it was reinforced by the defeat of 1918, for now German historians felt they had to defend the existence of their nation against a hostile world. For many non-German historians and commentators Prussia now looked like the villain of the piece in German history, a hotbed of militarism and illiberalism. Her predominance after 1870 had foisted these characteristics on the whole of Germany. By the time of the Second World War historians and observers outside Germany often saw the course of German history as tending towards an idolisation of the state both at home and abroad. Hitler was regarded as the outcome of tendencies sometimes taken as far back as Luther. The work of A.J.P. Taylor is a well-known example of such a view.

After 1945 German historians had themselves to come to terms with the fact that what they had for so long praised as the noble climax of their national story had turned into a nightmare of destruction and crime. Initially, many of them took the view that National Socialism had been an aberration, a turning away from normal traditions due to exceptionally unfavourable circumstances. There was a tendency to put much emphasis on the personality of Hitler and to see him almost as an evil invader from outer space. The tradition in German historiography to emphasise political and diplomatic history, in line with the primacy of foreign policy, and to stress the importance of personality in history facilitated this approach.

A New Generation of German Historians

In the 1960s the writing of their own history by German historians underwent a major change. First the Hamburg historian, Fritz Fischer, in a book translated as *Germany's Aims in the First World War,* documented the strength of the pressure for hegemony and expansion in Germany before the First World War. This ran counter to the contention, to the making of which the German historical profession had devoted a great deal of effort even before 1933, that Germany had little or no responsibility for the outbreak of war in 1914. The continuity between the aims of traditional German nationalism and those of Hitler emerged all too clearly.

The younger generation of German historians, who came to the fore in the 1960s, no longer tainted with any personal association with the Third Reich, were very concerned to trace the roots of National Socialism in German society. They moved away from the concentration by their predecessors on political and diplomatic history and sought historical causes in social and economic structures. Arguments about the disjuncture between relative political backwardness compared with a rapidly evolving modern industrial structure were advanced. The theory of a German *Sonderweg* (see page 2) took a new turn. Whereas in the past it had been seen as a mark of German superiority to the West, it now became a term for German backwardness and failure. The methods by which a German national state came into existence and the way it was governed were regarded by historians such as H.-U. Wehler, most comprehensively in his book *The German Empire 1871-1918*, as deeply damaging and stunting to the development of a vigorous democratic, libertarian consciousness. There has, in the meantime, been some reaction against these views. The imperial era is no longer seen in an unrelieved negative light. The importance of personalities like Bismarck and Hitler is again emphasised more than it was by the social historians, but few would now argue that National Socialism can be explained without reference to many deep-seated trends in German society, going back at least to the nineteenth century.

Specific Controversies

Within these broad tendencies in the historiography of modern Germany, there are many specific interpretative controversies, which have already been referred to in these pages. Thus, there is the question to what extent Germany might have found her way to a more fully-fledged parliamentary democracy, but for the First World War, or was Imperial Germany heading for some kind of autocracy foreshadowing the Third Reich? Could more have been made of the upheavals of 1918/19 to lay firmer foundations for democracy? How weak was the political and economic position of the Weimar Republic even in its best years? Were there alternatives to the policies of deflation in the early 1930s that might have limited the rise of political extremism? Could Hitler's appointment as Chancellor have been prevented even in the final weeks before January 1933? Lastly, there are the different approaches to the interpretation of the Third Reich: how totalitarian was it? What was the interaction between intention, the thrust of ideology, and structure, the opportunities and circumstances that shaped the course of events? How central a figure was Hitler?

The Value of Different Approaches

These questions have been raised and to some extent answered in the foregoing pages. By advancing different interpretative schemes it is possible to gain greater insight into what happened. Historical hypotheses help to find a way through the otherwise almost impenetrable jungle of facts. Different hypotheses are not mutually exclusive. The student needs to be aware of them, but there is no need to come down on one side or the other. Taking the arguments about the Third Reich as an example, the perception that it was not a monolith, that in fact it was an exceptionally unco-ordinated set-up, has added greatly to our understanding. That even such an apparently planned undertaking as the murder of European Jews developed in a haphazard fashion and to some extent from the bottom up is now generally accepted. This does not mean that Hitler was either a weak dictator or did not intend such an outcome, or was not essential in bringing it about. Students in answering examination questions or essays should, therefore, show awareness that different or even contrasting interpretative approaches are possible, are valid and help to shed light on the complex course of history.

11 Germany 1916-1941. Continuity and Change

From Unification to Reunification

When the Second World War ended in 1945 with the total collapse of the Third Reich, this became known in Germany as Zero Hour (*Stunde Null*). Little was left of the Reich that Bismarck had established 75 years earlier, but history never wipes the slate completely clean. After 1948 when, for the second time in a generation, a new currency was introduced, though this time only in that part of Germany controlled by the Western powers, a rapid economic recovery, often called an economic miracle, took place in Western Germany. One important legacy had in fact survived from the Bismarckian Reich: Germany was still a highly industrialised country, with a highly skilled population.

When, after the lapse of another forty years, the East German Communist regime collapsed and Germany was reunited in 1990, it was again the most populous country in Europe west of Russia. It is a smaller country in terms of territory, for the provinces east of the Oder-Neisse line (see map, page 135) are no longer part of it. Most of the Germans who lived in these areas were expelled at the end of the Second World War, another tragic result of Hitler's destructive activities. The Federal Republic of Germany is in many ways a model democracy and has never regarded itself as in the line of succession of previous Reichs. The term Reich, or empire, with its universal and limitless claims is far removed from the minds of the Germans of the present day. No one now seriously expects the Germany of the present to make another attempt to dominate Europe militarily.

Germany in Europe

Even when Germany was at the height of her drive for power before and during the First World War, the more moderate nationalists, men like Bethmann Hollweg, envisaged German predominance to be, in the main, informal and based on economic pre-eminence. She would remain part of the international economic system. The more extreme annexationists, for example Ludendorff, envisaged a self-sufficient empire incorporating large tracts of territory in Western and even more in Eastern Europe. During the Weimar period the policy of Stresemann, a thoroughly realistic politician, was based on the restoration of Germany's status as a great power through her economic strength. This could only take place within the political and economic community of Western nations, and not through military aggression. Hitler's ideas were exactly the opposite. His was the most extreme version of empire, based on the permanent acquisition of Lebensraum and the enslavement or expulsion of the native population from the conquered territories. Some people even now fear that an informal German economic predominance in Europe could become a reality unless strong institutions of a united Europe supersede the separate nation states.

To point out continuities about the German situation in Europe does not mean that history is at all likely to repeat itself. It merely illustrates that there are some continuities in the problem of accommodating a powerful German state in Europe. It is one of the reasons why there has been a strong drive for European unification since 1945, for some form of European unity seemed to many the only way of achieving such an accommodation in a manner satisfactory to all. European unity also found strong support in Germany after 1945, as a way of moral rehabilitation and regaining acceptance in the family of nations. It was a vision of the future different from the nation state for which Germany as well as Europe paid so high a price in blood and destruction. In West Germany after 1945 there was a widespread feeling that nationalism had reached the end of the road and that in future the loyalty of Germans should be to their democratic constitution rather than to a nation which had ceased to exist. It remains to be seen whether these sentiments will survive, now that a united German nation has again come into being. In the past there was always a feeling in Germany that their culture and outlook on life differed from and was superior to that of the Western democracies, France, Britain and America. It is a hopeful sign that almost all Germans now feel their nation to be an integral part of the West.

Continuity and Change in Germany's Domestic Situation

Few commentators now doubt that the Germany that came after the Zero Hour of 1945 is very different from what existed before. As we have seen Hitler and the Nazis saw themselves as the world's greatest revolutionaries, who would create a new society that would last a thousand years. The racial state they intended to establish would be based on values in most respects the opposite of those previously prevailing in the civilisation of the West. Fortunately, the total defeat of National Socialism, moral as well as physical, wiped out virtually all trace of its destructive and evil schemes. Occasional attempts in Germany to revive Nazism under some new label have never come to much.

The question therefore arises in what way German society since 1945 has been different from that which went before. As we have seen (see page 2), historians have argued that Germany developed along lines somewhat different from that of the Western democracies, particularly Britain.

Although the theory of a German *Sonderweg* is debatable, none would dispute that there was a weakness of liberalism, parliamentarism and democracy, which eventually facilitated the rise of Nazism.

The Third Reich - A Social Revolution?

If, therefore, German society is now different from what it was before 1945, we must ask how this has come about. The revolution which Hitler intended to make, failed. Even in the 1930s the groups whom the Nazis particularly meant to favour, for example farmers, small businessmen and craftsmen, did not fare very well. In spite of all the propaganda about *Volksgemeinschaft*, there was no redistribution of property nor even greater equality of incomes (see page 115). The need to maximise production for war favoured the large corporations. They were best placed to exploit the conquest of territory and the recruitment of slave labour. Their record in this respect still causes embarrassment from time to time in the present day.

The establishment of the Third Reich was, however, a great political upheaval and encouraged social mobility. Existing elites found their influence reduced or had to seek to maintain it by joining the Nazi party and its formations. Ambitious men from all sections of society sought a rank in the SS, seen as the new elite organisation of the Nazi state. Even greater changes came about as a result of war, defeat and the movement of refugees and expellees after the war, the greatest migration of peoples in Europe since the end of the Roman Empire. It was estimated in 1966 that over 10 million people of the 60 million population of West Germany, as it then was, were expellees from the territories east of the Oder-Neisse line and from elsewhere in Eastern Europe. Many more millions were refugees from East Germany. Movements of population on such a scale change societies profoundly.

The revolution the Nazis intended to make failed, but the sheer destruction they wrought caused huge upheavals in German society. As we have seen, the Junkers, the Prussian aristocracy mainly from the provinces east of the Elbe, were very powerful in the Second Reich and continued to exercise an anti-republican influence in the Weimar period. Those who did not succumb to Hitler's drastic revenge after the failed attempt on his life on 20 July 1944 were wiped out by the expulsions after 1945 and by the expropriations in the Communist East German Republic. This is just one example of the profound changes that have taken place in German society. The year 1945 was also another political watershed, though the programme of de-Nazification started by the Allies never got very far. Too many Germans were implicated in the Nazi regime to make a thorough purge feasible and the beginnings of the Cold War halted the process in West Germany. In East Germany the establishment and eventual collapse of the Communist regime caused further upheavals.

The Modernisation of German Society

The rise of National Socialism was in part a protest against the pains and perils of modernity. The process of industrialisation and urbanisation in Germany was, after unification in 1870, so rapid that society and its institutions experienced difficulties of adjustments. Those sections of the population that felt themselves to be losers in the process were particularly prone to the attractions of extreme nationalism, racism and later Nazism. Up to 1918 the political framework of the country was, to some extent, out of phase with its social and economic structure. The Weimar political system, more adequate to the modernised state of German society, was, because of its origins in defeat, never fully accepted.

National Socialism was backward looking, in its nostalgia for a society based on a healthy Germanic farming race, in its attitude to women and in many other respects. Its techniques of mass manipulation, propaganda and terror were very modern. The drive for rearmament and towards war meant that the Nazis had to discard many of their own anti-modern ideas and policies. Finally war, defeat and its consequences subjected Germany to such drastic upheavals that many obstacles to modernity simply disappeared. Even though there is continuity about some aspects of Germany's history, particularly those connected with her geographical situation, the upheavals caused by the Third Reich, the Second World War and its aftermath have also brought about profound changes and much discontinuity.

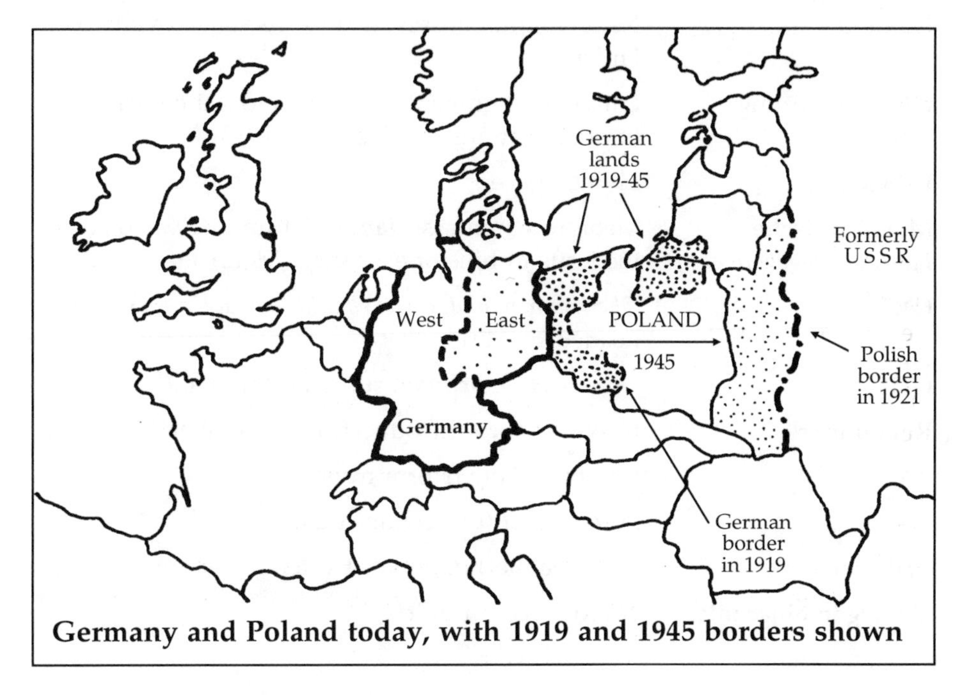

Germany and Poland today, with 1919 and 1945 borders shown

Glossary

Anschluss	Literally 'joining', the term given to Austria joining the Reich, a possibility since 1918, realised in March 1938.
Auswärtiges Amt	The German Foreign Office.
Bekennende Kirche	Confessing Church, formed in 1934, the Lutherans opposing Nazi policies in their churches.
Burgfriede	Political truce in 1914.
Einsatzgruppen	Special SS forces charged with the elimination of ideological and racial opponents, especially in Poland and Russia.
Erbhofsgesetz	Nazi law of 1933 to keep farms in the family.
Führerprinzip	Leadership principle, the Führer has the ultimate authority.
Gauleiter	Nazi regional bosses, tied by personal loyalty to Hitler.
Gleichschaltung	Literally 'alignment', co-ordination, the take-over of organisations by Nazism in 1933.
Lebensraum	Living space.
Metallurgische ***Forschungsgesellschaft***	Metal research association, set up in 1934 to cover the issue of bills of exchange (Mefo).
OKW	*Oberkommando der Wehrmacht,* set up in 1938, headed by Hitler.
OHL	*Oberste Heeresleitung,* supreme command.
Rentenmark	New currency introduced in November 1923.
SA	*Sturmabteilung* (storm troop).
SS	*Schutzstaffel* (protection squad).
Stahlhelm	(Steel helmet) nationalist veterans' organisation.
Volksgemeinschaft	National community.

The Main Political Parties of the Weimar Republic

DDP (Deutsche Demokratische Partei), German Democratic Party, the left liberal party founded in 1918, the successor of the Progressives of the imperial period. Represented teachers, other professionals, farmers in some areas, but after a strong showing in 1919 declined rapidly.

DNVP (Deutschnationale Volkspartei), German National People's Party, successor of the conservative parties of the empire. Its main strength was in Protestant regions, especially in the eastern provinces of Prussia. In the early years of the republic it also included most of the Völkische (racialists). It reached its peak in 1924, but in the closing years of Weimar most of its support went to the Nazis. It was in the coalition cabinet, formed by Hitler in 1933, but this did not save it from extinction a few months later.

DVP (Deutsche Volkspartei), German People's Party, the right-wing liberal party, founded by Stresemann when the DDP rejected him in 1918. Successor to the National Liberals of the imperial period. Represented industry and commerce. Picked up support from the DDP in 1920, but then also declined.

KPD (Kommunistische Partei Deutschlands), the Communist Party, founded in 1919, from the Spartakus League and other organisations of the extreme left. Increasingly aligned with the Soviet Union and Stalin after 1920.

NSDAP (Nationalsozialistische Deutsche Arbeiterpartei), the Nazi Party, in full the National Socialist German Workers Party.

SPD (Sozialdemokratische Partei Deutschlands), the Social Democratic Party of Germany, nicknamed Sozis (Nazis was a similar abbreviation). Founded in 1875, it was the largest socialist party in Europe before 1914 and the party most closely identified with the Weimar Republic.

USPD (Unabhängige Sozialdemokratische Partei Deutschlands), Independent Social Democratic Party, split off from the SPD as an anti-war party in 1917. By 1922 most of the leaders rejoined the SPD, while most of the voters went to the KPD. The party declined into insignificance.

Zentrum, the Catholic Centre Party, which came into existence during the Bismarck era in opposition to his anti-Catholic policies. In 1920 the Bavarian wing split off and became the Bayerische Volkspartei (BVP, Bavarian People's Party), but the two wings did not put up candidates against each other. The two parties retained most of their strength throughout the Weimar period. The Centre was one of the main supports of the republic, forming with the SPD and the DDP the so-called Weimar coalition.

Further Reading

1. General Textbooks covering the whole period:

William Carr, *A History of Germany 1815-1990* (Edward Arnold, 4th edn., 1992). Volker Berghahn, *Modern Germany* (Cambridge University Press, 2nd edn., 1987) - contains extensive statistical tables. Gordon Craig, *Germany 1866-1945* (Oxford University Press, 1981) - a fuller, narrative treatment. Mary Fulbrook, *The Divided Nation. Fontana History of Germany 1918-1990* (1991) - a succinct survey.

2. Imperial Germany:

H.-U. Wehler, *The German Empire 1871-1918* (Berg, 1985) - the classical statement of the negative view. W.J. Mommsen, *Imperial Germany 1867-1918. Politics, Culture and Society in an Authoritarian State* (Edward Arnold, 1995) - a collection of translated essays by one of the foremost German historians. Richard J. Evans (ed.), *Society and Politics in Wilhelmine Germany* (Croom Helm, 1978) - a collection of essays by various authors.

3. The Weimar Period:

E.J. Feuchtwanger, *From Weimar to Hitler: Germany 1918-33* (Macmillan, 2nd edn., 1995) - the most recent general treatment in English. Eberhard Kolb, *The Weimar Republic* (Unwin and Hyman, 1988) - translated from the German, includes review of historiography. Ian Kershaw (ed.), *Weimar: Why did German democracy fail?* (Weidenfeld and Nicolson, 1990) - a collection of essays.

4. The Third Reich:

Norbert Frei, *National Socialist Rule in Germany. The Führer State 1933-1945* (Blackwell, 1993) - translation of a recent German succinct treatment mainly of domestic developments. Ian Kershaw, *The Nazi Dictatorship. Problems and Perspectives of Interpretation* (Edward Arnold, 3rd edn., 1993) - a review of interpretations and historiography. Michael Burleigh and Wolfgang Wippermann, *The Racial State. Germany 1933-1945* (Cambridge University Press, 1991) - deals with the implementation of the Nazi racial doctrines.

Index